WHAT LEADERS ARE SAYING ABOUT GUTENBERG TO GOOGLE

There is no pastoral leadership skill that will substitute for the effective preaching and teaching of the Word of God. Style in communication is important, but however useful drama or media may be, or colorful delivery be enhancing, they cannot replace the exposition of the Scripture or the anointing of the Holy Spirit. James Davis is an excellent advocate for the scope of values and perception significant to unite the Spirit and the Word with guidance for reaching, touching and affecting the hearts, minds and souls of our contemporary culture.

> Dr. Jack W. Hayford
> Chancellor, The King's College & Seminary
> Founding Pastor, The Church On The Way

This new powerful resource will help ministers become powerful preachers of the Word of God. James O. Davis has taken his life, education, and ministry to form a template for success in pulpit ministry. Use this sound wisdom to improve your preaching, and let's get on with winning people to Christ each and every week.

> Bishop Charles Blake
> Presiding Bishop, Church of God in Christ
> Founding Pastor, West Angeles Church of God in Christ
> Los Angeles, California

James O. Davis has written the quintessential book on preaching. I recommend this valuable resource to those who wish to create, connect and communicate the gospel. Read it and reap from it!

> Dr. Raymond Culpepper
> General Overseer, Church of God
> Cleveland, Tennessee

In the last ten to fifteen years, a digital divide has arisen between the presenter and the listener worldwide. James O. Davis presents the pastor with a preaching process to connect Googlers with the Gospel. Just take a look at the chapter titles, and you will know you are holding in your hand a unique, cutting-edge book for twenty-first century biblical preaching. Get the book, read the book, and apply it to God's glory!

Dr. Ronnie W. Floyd
Senior Pastor, First Baptist Church of Springdale and
The Church at Pinnacle Hills
Springdale, Arkansas

James O. Davis is a man who understands the creative process and dynamic relationship that it takes to captivate your audience in the twenty-first century. His challenging message, relevant knowledge, in-depth research, and heart for the Kingdom of God will resource and inspire any passionate preacher.

Rev. Brian Houston
Senior Pastor, Hillsong Church
Sydney, Australia

If you are not communicating, then you are not connecting. If we are not connecting, then there will be fewer conversions. It is paramount that every proclaimer of the Gospel know how to reach Gutenbergers and Googlers with the Gospel. In his latest book, Dr. James O. Davis gives to us the crossover laws of communication which result in maximum impact to our listeners. Be sure to secure a copy as soon as possible!

Dr. Marcus Lamb
President/CEO, Daystar
Fort Worth, Texas

One of the greatest challenges today is to communicate effectively in the digital age. James O. Davis powerfully reveals the systematic steps required to connect audiences worldwide. This is a timely treasure for us as we seek to equip more pastors than ever to effectively preach the Gospel.

Dr. James Leggett
General Overseer, International Pentecostal Holiness
Oklahoma City, Oklahoma

With each generation comes the responsibility to equip emerging pastors to communicate to the current culture. James O. Davis has systematically developed a successful process for both young and seasoned preachers to develop and deploy life-changing presentations.

Dr. Stan Toler
General Superintendent, Church of the Nazarene

James O. Davis gives practical answers and spiritual observations and helpful suggestions to improve the cuisine and menus of the pulpit. This work is a how-to manual for the spiritual chef who sincerely desires to feed the sheep of God. Davis may have indeed produced the premier manual for preaching in a Google world.

Bishop Kenneth C. Ulmer
Presiding Bishop, Macedonia International Bible Fellowship
President, Kings College and Seminary
Los Angeles, California

Gutenberg to Google by Dr. James O. Davis is an incredible resource for pastors and others interested in more effectively communicating the Gospel! Drawing on more than twenty-five years of evangelistic preaching, teaching, and lecturing, Davis presents time-tested tools for preachers to demonstrate the Bible's relevance to a digital world. I'm thrilled about this new book. Those who use Davis' "Laws of Communication" will be helped in closing the gap between the digital world and the timeless Word of God."

Dr. R. Lamar Vest
President and CEO, American Bible Society

Pastors are struggling as never before to connect and communicate with the emerging generation. James O. Davis has taken a wealth of lifetime learning and distilled it into these few pages where he explains, expounds, and expands the creative process to cross the twenty-first century digital divide. I believe this will help any pastor who desires to bring life-changing presentations for the fulfillment of the Great Commission.

Dr. George O. Wood
General Superintendent, Assemblies of God
Springfield, Missouri

Victory is always on the other side of a fight. Today, our world needs ministers who are willing to fight for justice, righteousness, and faith. James O. Davis has crafted a powerful weapon to help in the fight. In an era of vainglory, cheap celebrity and insipid thought-shapers who decry the historically-proven Biblical standards of right or wrong, it is time to reshape the generations that are coming into the image of Christ, His character, lifestyle and essence. God's message of hope for the world is His power contained in the hearts of men and women of faith – allies committed to truth, honor and the presence of God in every arena of culture.

Rev. Paul Louis Cole
President, Christian Men's Network Worldwide

Very few leaders have the ability to network both young and older leaders worldwide. In James O. Davis' newest book, he reveals the laws communicating to any audience worldwide. Read it! Reflect on it and receive its benefits for a lifetime!

Dr. Gustavo Crocker
Church of the Nazarene Eurasia Director
Switzerland

From years of training, study, research, observation, and experience, James O. Davis has gleaned nuggets of truth and placed them within the reach of any minister desiring to improve. His ability to analyze where we are today in relation to our culture and society is of extreme value to anyone who is serious about connecting with the present generation.

Rev. Billy Joe Daugherty
Senior Pastor, Victory Christian Center
Tulsa, Oklahoma

Thank God for insights like those of James O. Davis in this timely book that will help equip emerging pastors to be powerfully effective communicators of Christ's Good News. It should be required reading in every Bible school and seminary committed to raising up effective preachers and teachers of the gospel.

Dr. Dick Eastman
International President, Every Home for Christ
Colorado Springs, Colorado

James O. Davis has given practical and powerful insights to every pastor who wishes his messages had a powerful impact upon his or her listeners. This book comes at a critical time when we desperately need to connect the emerging generation of Googlers. In the years ahead, this valuable resource will become known as one of the paramount books on preaching throughout the world.

Dr. Des Evans
Bethesda Community Church
Fort Worth, Texas

In the last twenty-five years, James O. Davis has brought more than 7,000 presentations in nearly one hundred nations. He reveals the powerful process of connecting Googlers with the Gospel. I recommend this valuable resource to those who wish to create, connect and communicate the gospel. It is the premiere book on preaching today!

Rev. Leon Fontaine
Founding Pastor, Springs Church
Winnipeg, Canada

In the years ahead, this valuable resource will become known as one of the paramount books on preaching throughout the world. Be sure to acquire a copy today!

Dr. J. Don George
Senior Pastor, Calvary Church
Irving, Texas

Having been a preacher and a pastor for more than forty years, how I wish someone would have told me what you have presented in your book. But still, it's never too late. Therefore, regardless of how long you have been a preacher or a pastor, James O. Davis' book is a resource all preachers and pastors should read.

Dr. Prince Guneratnam
General Superintendent-Emeritus, Assemblies of God of Malaysia
Senior Pastor, Calvary Church
Kuala Lumpur, Malaysia

Gutenberg to Google will prove valuable reading to anyone who is charged with teaching and preaching the Word of God. Dr. James O. Davis provides an outstanding biblical and practical process that will help you and your pastoral team to "rightly divide" and "rightly deliver" a changeless Gospel to changing culture.

Dr. Ademola Ishola
General Secretary, Nigerian Baptist Convention
Lagos, Nigeria

We must equip those who are responsible for giving solid Biblical expositions of the Word of God as we fulfill the Great Commission of our Lord to go and to disciple all nations. As Dr. Davis states so well, "Regardless of how dynamic ministers make their presentations, they will never be as effective as the Word of God. When they cause people to read the Word of God, the Word of God reads them." May God's servants capture this truth and the other nineteen indispensable laws of communication. I highly recommend this most needed treasure for God's men and women at this most critical moment in the history of the announcement of the Gospel and in the time of the tremendous chaos among the nations.

Dr. Walter C. Kaiser Jr.
Colman M. Mockler Emeritus Professor of Old Testament
President Emeritus, Gordon-Conwell Theological Seminary

God is raising pastors and planters worldwide. These leaders need to be equipped and empowered to proclaim the gospel in ever culture. *Gutenberg to Google*, Dr. James O. Davis shows how to biblically and practically communicate effectively to the emerging Google generation. I am thrilled, finally, there is a cutting-edge resource that connects Gutenberg and Google worlds with the Gospel. You will find this valuable resource to be one of the most powerful preaching resources of the twenty-first century.

Rev. Suliasi Kurulo
Founding Pastor, World Harvest Centre
Suva, Fiji

Being able to communicate to any audience is rare in this rapidly changing world. James O. Davis has written a masterpiece for ministers who wish to bring powerful presentations to change lives anywhere. Dr. Davis' book is a must-read book for pastors throughout the world today.

Rev. Eddy Leo
Founder, Abba Love Ministries
Jakarta, Indonesia

James O. Davis teaches both the young and seasoned presenter how to energize any audience for productive life changes. I highly recommend this invaluable resource to every leader who wishes to increase their level of influence in the world today.

Dr. Ben Lerner
Founder, Maximized Living Foundation
Orlando, Florida

I have witnessed firsthand Dr. James O. Davis' love for people and his unique ability to identify with the audience and to share in-depth information in easy to understand fashion. Dr. Davis has now chosen to share with us in this remarkable book the secrets of creativity, the power of vision-casting, the keys to effective invitations, the dynamics of delivery and much more. Read it, digest it, share it, and increase your ability to communicate.

Dr. Douglas LeRoy
General Director, Church of God World Missions
Cleveland, Tennessee

"Without proper communication, there will not be motivation! James Davis has provided a profound communicator's guide to crossing and connecting with today's listener. Leaders worldwide have exclaimed, 'It is the most essential book to captivating and challenges audiences everywhere to become followers of Christ.' Get it today!"

Mr. Peter Lowe
Founder, Get Motivated!

Dr. James O. Davis has the ability to communicate to different cultures worldwide. He reveals the essential laws of effectively preaching to virtually any audience. Having had the privilege of experiencing his ministry firsthand, I highly recommend this invaluable resource to you. Once you have understood and applied these powerful laws, your communication will never be the same!

Dr. John Ed Mathison
President, John Ed Mathison Leadership Institute
Pastor Emeritus, Frazier Memorial United Methodist
Montgomery, Alabama

Whatever else a preacher does in the twenty-first century he must effectively communicate. To communicate effectively he must do so in a creative way that connects with today's savvy listener. James O. Davis' latest book is just the ticket to enable today's pastor to break barriers and to build bridges to an Internet generation that needs to hear God's truth more than ever.

Dr. James Merritt
Cross-Point Church
Atlanta, Georgia

For more than fifteen years, James O. Davis and I have been working together in India. When he comes to our nation, our pastors thoroughly enjoy his preaching ministry. He understands the mindset of our leaders in particular and of listeners in general. This valuable resource is destined to raise the level of communicating the gospel worldwide.

Dr. David Mohan
General Superintendent, Assemblies of God
Madras, India

The Global world has emerged with the Google generation. As pastors it is imperative that we continue to learn ways and have keys to connect and communicate to stay relative to a changing world. James O. Davis as a master craftsman hands us those keys in his latest ground breaking book. All who want to be effective in reaching the lost, extending the Kingdom of God through the preached word – this book is a must-read book!

Rev. Peter Mortlock
Senior Pastor, City Impact Church
Auckland, New Zealand

With more demands placed on the pastor today than in any previous generation, practical ministry resources based on years of experience are needed for maximum productivity. James O. Davis further equips the pastor to minimize time, maximize quality, and multiply results. I highly recommend that you acquire this invaluable resource and begin reaping the benefits immediately!

Dr. Gary Smalley
Founder, Smalley Relationship Center
Branson, Missouri

Dr. James O. Davis has traveled throughout the earth for more than twenty-five years, communicating to different cultures in almost one hundred nations. In his latest book, Dr. Davis teaches the reader the creative secrets of communication, the winning vocal techniques, the keys to effective invitations, the dynamics of delivery and so much more. I challenge every preacher who yearns to have their altars filled with new converts to read this cutting edge resource.

Dr. David Sobrepena
Founding Pastor, Word of Hope
Manila, Philippines

Communication is paramount in every endeavor, especially in the preaching of the Gospel to those who desperately need to know Christ. Dr. James O. Davis has powerfully given to us the frequencies required to awakening our audiences to the greatest news in the world today. I encourage you to digest these laws so that you will be able to deliver impacting messages.

Rev. John Sorensen
President, Evangelism Explosion International
Fort Lauderdale, Florida

If there was ever a preacher who should write a book on preaching, it is James O. Davis. Not only did he complete his doctorate and write his project on preaching, he himself is a great preacher who has preached in some of the greatest churches in the world. I don't know of any one individual who has preached in more great churches than Davis. In this book he puts life into preaching, and helps you to put your life into your preaching.

Dr. Elmer Towns
Co-founder, Liberty University
Lynchburg, Virginia

With each generation comes the responsibility to equip emerging expositors to help fulfill the Great Commission. I highly recommend Gutenberg to Google to every preacher who wishes to stay on the cutting edge of culture.

Dr. Paul L. Walker
Director of Local Church Development
Church of God, Cleveland, Tennessee

Preaching primarily seeks to communicate, connecting heaven to earth. The effective preacher is an effective communicator. No more, no less. Dr. Davis, one of the great communicators of our time, provides hands-on tools that all communicators need if they are going to be effective. This book is a must-read.

Rev. Isaac Wheigar
Wesleyan General Overseer
Monrovia, Liberia

Gutenberg

To

Google:

The Twenty Indispensable Laws of Communication

James O. Davis

A Billion Soul® Book

Word & Spirit Resources
Tulsa, OK

Gutenberg

To

Google:

Gutenberg To Google: The Twenty Indispensable Laws of Communication

Copyright © 2009 James O. Davis

ISBN: 978-0-9842534-9-4

Word & Spirit Resources
P. O. Box 701403
Tulsa, OK 74170

A BILLION SOUL® BOOK
Billion Soul®
P. O. Box 411605
Melbourne, FL 32941-1605

James O. Davis
P. O. Box 560577
Viera, FL 32956
www.JamesODavis.org
www.Billion.tv

DEDICATION

This book is dedicated to Sheri Reneé Davis,
who has walked with me through the mornings,
mid-days, and midnight hours of the challenges of ministry.
She has witnessed firsthand the sun rising over sermonizing
and the sun setting with souls coming to Christ.

ACKNOWLEDGEMENTS

Heartfelt thanks to leaders who have been both sounding boards and spring boards for this timely book project. These world-class leaders serve hand-in-hand and shoulder-to-shoulder in the Billion Soul Network.

CONTENTS

FOREWORD

This current generation of biblical preachers has witnessed and experienced more change in a shorter period of time than any previous generation in modern history. No wonder the world of homiletics is reeling. As we assess the future formation of church pioneers, planters, and preachers, one thing is clear: we must be equipped to cross successfully the "3G bridge" of communication.

The 3G bridge of communication is the ability to move from the "Gutenberg World" of the printing press to the "Google World" of the Internet without compromising the Gospel. Preachers are commissioned not only to exegete the words of Scripture but to exegete the images and metaphors that God chose to reveal the divine to the human.

In this book, James O. Davis has provided a guidepost to transformational preaching in the 21st century. During the completion of this technological transition from analogue to digital, communicators are challenged with the complexity of connecting with the audience so that, as Jesus put it, "none shall perish but all have everlasting life" (John 3:16).

James O. Davis has carefully and creatively shared the bridge-building components to help us to connect and communicate to "Gutenbergers" and "Googlers" worldwide. Over the last twenty-five years, he has given more than 7,000 life-changing presentations in more than 2,000 different locations to more than 5 million people face-to-face in more than 90 nations. I have personally witnessed him get off a plane from half a planet away and, without missing a beat or taking a break, deliver a powerful message that brought me to tears and ushered many in the congregation to the altar.

Davis' twenty indispensable "laws" are vital to the health and growth of the global church. If they are missing in your unveiling of the text, you may convey the "meaning of it," but your congregation may not leave "meaning it." It is through these "communication laws" that the church can maintain the critical balance between an unchanging content and changing cultural containers.

The Bible was written not to put the lives of people into print but to put "life" into people. That's the meaning of "in-spiration." The "in-spired" Word was brought to life by God's breathing out and our breathing in. The breath of God moved upon the writers, like it had originally moved upon the waters, and the "spirations" of the Spirit "in" them birthed the Holy Scriptures. The words of the Bible issued from a partnership between the breath of God and the hand of man.

The challenge preachers face today is in knowing how to "inhale" effectively the breathings of the Spirit and then to "exhale" the Word of God through dynamic life-giving experiences of the Word so people can live again. The Twenty Indispensable Laws is one of the most compelling and creative books on preaching in recent times. I challenge you to read it and bring a new dynamic power to your preaching, whether you are reaching out to the Gutenberg or Google worlds!

Leonard Sweet, PhD
April, 2009

INTRODUCTION

It was a beautiful summer evening with a clear sky in the Northern United States, the kind of evening that people from that area wait all year to enjoy. My wife, Sheri, and I were in nonstop motion in the constant buzz of a huge convention, enjoying vibrant ministry relationships and catching up with lifelong friends. One evening we walked into the cavernous arena for the general session and found seats among the 12,000 attendees who congregated at one end, the rest of the massive auditorium being curtained off. We were all eager to hear the possibilities of spiritual awakening and revival throughout the United States and the world. Months of planning, saving, calling ahead to connect with friends, packing clothes, and then hours of travel had finally brought us to this warm, wonderful, fun-filled, and friend-filled evening.

As we settled in, we smiled and waved across the auditorium to familiar faces and thumbed through the program. Along with our friends seated around us, we noted the time the evening would draw to a close. Many people would leave immediately to pick up their children in a separate building. Others, like us, would linger and find friends with whom to eat a late dinner.

Nowhere did I pick up the signals that I was about to endure hours of embarrassing agony and witness a communication meltdown of such proportion that it would leave an indelible mark on my life. On that beautiful summer evening, in one of the worst programs I have ever seen, I found myself committing to learn and apply dynamic principles of communication in my ministry life, the result of which you now hold in your hand.

That evening, the crowd's excitement was palpable, but it waned through preliminaries that dragged with what seemed endless monotony. The keynote presenter finally took the stage with just twenty minutes left on the schedule. Our stomachs were growling, and nervous parents were checking the time. Yet, the presenter chose to give a wooden presentation, including reading statistics with no visuals, that continued for an unmerciful hour and twenty minutes.

There was one interesting part of the evening, which was to watch the crowd. At first, parents walked out by two's with evident concern for the time and disinterest in hearing more droning statistics. Then, individuals started to dart into the aisles to escape. Finally, as if orchestrated by wedding ushers, whole rows of people began to stand up and clog the aisles in a mass exodus. By the time the presentation ended, I surveyed the crowd and estimated that perhaps one thousand of us remained. We were scattered so sparsely throughout that great auditorium that a shotgun blast may not have hit two people.

As ministers, we feel the keen pain of watching people who emotionally and spiritually leave our presentation even while physically sitting in our building. I have witnessed this all over the world, how people can check out with disinterest in what we have to say about Christ, His Church, and eternity. I have become convinced of what I learned in my first year of seminary, that it is a sin to bore people with the Gospel. What is more amazing than more than 11,000 people walking out was the presenter who kept going on and on despite the "second greatest exodus" since Moses led the Israelites out of Egypt!

For those who bring professional presentations, it is equally important to understand, apply, and execute the finest presentations possible to be the best representatives of our Lord even in a secular setting. Presentations may be seen live, on video, heard digitally or even via telephone call. Regardless of the means or even the purpose of communication, compounding laws of return occur when our vibrant message is sowed into the fertile soil of the minds of people.

You will not have to turn another page to learn your first lesson. Let me tell you what we do in the situation I saw that evening. Take the mic with a huge shot of high level energy and ask that no one leave. Ask members of the audience to look at their watches, and tell them that not only will you not go over the allotted time, but you will land it early, if they will just give you their attention for fifteen minutes. Then start with your most important point first, since you have had hours to reduce your presentation to its barest elements. Next, give them something to do: take out their pen, write it down, repeat it to their neighbor, laugh, yell the main point back to you, anything to rekindle their enthusiasm. Finally, announce that the statistics will become available by handout, online, or by mail if they will provide you an address. Then thank them for listening and sit down. Let me tell you, the presenter would have received a standing ovation from 12,000 grateful people!

After studying with some of the best communicators on the planet, speaking in front of every kind of crowd imaginable in multiplied hundreds of cultures and situations, and committing to improve each and every week through thousands of presentations over a quarter century, I have learned something!

Besides these culture variations worldwide, the global Church is riding the wave of the greatest technological shift in the history of humankind. The greatest advancement in language communication since the Gutenberg press made the Bible available to everyone 500 years ago is the Internet that is making virtually everything available to everyone. The emerging world of the Googlers is far different than that of the Gutenbergers. The Gutenberg generation is finding it hard to communicate with the Google generation and vice versa. As the Gutenberg generation passes from the scene over the next twenty to twenty-five years, the Gospel has to be placed in the hands and hearts of the Google generation. This may seem easy at first, but statistically the chasm of misconnect is widening with the present generation not hearing and understanding the Gospel.

These "Twenty Indispensable Laws of Communication" have been tried, tested, and found trustworthy worldwide. These laws will help you to build bridges between Gutenbergers and Googlers while at the same time, depending on your age, help you to communicate with Gutenbergers and Googlers directly. My prayer is that these communication laws will revolutionize your effectiveness as they have mine over the last twenty-five years. We are called and commanded to preach and present The Greatest Story Ever Told, the wondrous and awe-inspiring Gospel of our Lord Jesus Christ.

Left Brain
(Principles/Rational)

Right Brain
(Pictures/Relational)

LAW

1

FILL THE PULPIT AND LET GOD FILL THE BUILDING

How will they believe in Him whom they have not heard?
And how will they hear without a preacher?
How will they preach unless they are sent? (Rom 10:14-15)

For people to respond to the glorious Gospel, they must first understand it. Scientific research has uncovered much regarding how we think and digest information. As ministers of the Gospel, we depend on the power of the Holy Spirit. We also need to understand our audience to increase our level of effectiveness. Starting with Law One, we will build bridges between the relational and rational, the imagery and instructional, the pictures and the principles.

Over the years, I have been privileged to sit under some of the great communicators of the last century. One of them, the late Dr. James D. Brown, former President of the Assemblies of God Theological Seminary, used to coach me using his big preaching voice that grew only slightly feeble through the years. He taught me an axiom which is the foundation for understanding the communicator's role today.

"James," Dr. Brown said on more than one occasion, "fill the pulpit and let God fill the building." He would often add, "You fulfill your role, and the Lord will take care of His role. If you commit to being an expositor of the Word of God, then you will never lack for an opportunity to minister."

claimed, a group on an expedition was rowing to shore. They agreed that the man who placed his hand on the shore first would become their leader. One of those men, O'Neil, rowed as fast as he could, but a stronger rower took the lead. When O'Neil realized that he was not going to possess the land first, he dropped the oars, seized a battle axe, chopped off one of his hands, and threw it to shore! He would rather lead with one hand than not lead at all.

I propose that if we do not possess this kind of red-hot passion to pursue the person of Christ and His promises, we may be preachers but will never become a "Man of God."

The "Man of God" Is Known by What He Fights For

The "Man of God" is a boxer, a wrestler, a soldier (1 Tim 6:12). He is engaged in war. When Paul said, "Fight the good fight," he was saying, "agonize the agony." Boxing during Greek times was done with fur-lined gloves on the inside, ox hide on the outside and filled with iron and lead. The loser had his eyes gouged out. We must have the courage of our convictions.

Most times, the Church does not know how to fight because we do not know how to think right. The Church cannot protect itself from outside forces because we have forgotten how to think. We are not wrestling against flesh and blood. We are fighting against error and we must win. We battle against the world, the flesh, the devil, sin, heresy, error, apathy, and lethargy in the Church.

We are called as soldiers to "keep the faith," to defend or keep the truth. We must get a grip on eternal life. We will not mind losing our life in this world if we have a firm grip on eternal life. We can be preachers and still not fully understand these truths. But, "Men of God" know why they are here and know how to execute a difference during their time on earth.

The "Man of God" Is Known for What He Is Faithful To

The commandment of Paul to Timothy refers to the whole of Scripture (1 Tim 6:13-14). The "Man of God" is charged in the presence of God—Who is the God of life, and Christ who was consistent and uncompromising with His own confession before Pilate—to keep the Word of God without staining it or bringing reproach upon it until the Second Coming of Christ.

We are commanded to guard what has been entrusted to us (1 Tim 6:20). We have to guard the sacred treasure. If we do not guard the treasure, we cannot be considered a "Man of God."

Some local churches operate as a merry-go-round, crowded with people sitting down on a seat they did not pay for, controlled by a man who has nothing to say, with a lot of up and down motion and beautiful music, but everyone gets off where they got on!

The "Man of God" is not known for how well he strokes the sheep, but how well he feeds them and protects them from the wolves.

Picture of Preaching

After we examine our lives, we must empower our commitments. Incarnation is the "picture" of preaching. Incarnation is the "inspiration of Scripture" in our world. The Bible is not meant merely to put the lives of people into print but to put "life" into the souls of people. Incarnation depends on inspiration. A person cannot have "the Word became flesh" without "breath." The term "inspiration" means "breath." "For no prophecy was ever made by an act of human will, but men moved by the Holy Spirit spoke from God" (2 Pet 1:21). "All Scripture is inspired by God" (2 Tim 3:16a) or is given by the "breath of God."

God breathed the words of the Bible. By His Spirit, God quickened the authors of the Bible to write His words for us. The breath of God moved upon them and through them in a manner that caused them to write down the words of God. The words in the Bible got there from the breath of God and the hand of man.

The challenge preachers face today is in knowing how to "inhale" correctly (exegesis) the breath of God or the Word of God. The goal is not just to get the Word of God into the preacher's head but into the preacher's heart. This is where the role of the Holy Spirit comes in as it relates to preaching. Do you know the difference between being a "professional preacher" and a "powerful preacher"?

After ministers have inhaled the breath of God and His Word, they are to "exhale" the Word of God through anointed preaching so people can live again. The minister can either share the inspired scriptures for information or incarnation. Just as the Holy Spirit birthed or conceived Jesus in Mary, preachers are to have the kind of anointed ministry that births Jesus in the lives of others.

Precepts of Preaching

We have to examine our calling, empower our commitments, and evaluate the culture around us. Powerful preaching impregnates people with the seed, the *spermos*—from which the term "sperm" is derived—the Word of God. Eternal life springs forth from impregnated hearts. The result is salvation through belief in Jesus Christ. That is how the "Word becomes flesh" today. People must experience the "new birth" of Jesus inside them to enter into salvation.

Whether we are Gutenbergers or Googlers, we are called to fill the pulpit and to cross the chasm of communication. We must know our times and be able to execute an eternal difference.

Whether we are Gutenbergers or Googlers, we are called to fill the pulpit and to cross the chasm of communication. We must know our times and be able to execute an eternal difference. Our world changes every week.

On October 11, 1998, Merrill Lynch ran full-page ads in many newspapers with the headline, "The World Is Ten Years Old." They were referring to the Berlin Wall coming down in 1989.

Some say there have been great changes in humanity approximately every 500 years. In 1492, there was a great upheaval. Everything began to change. Columbus proved that the world was not flat but round. Even though he was trying to go to China, he ran into North America, and the whole world changed forever.

Now, it has been more than 500 years since Columbus sailed the ocean. The Industrial Age is coming to a close, and the Information Age is taking over. Many historians use the fall of the Berlin Wall as the event that opened the floodgate of rapid change in our world.

When the Berlin Wall fell, the Cold War ended and globalization began. When the Berlin Wall came down, the World Wide Web went up. The rules changed.

During the Cold War, what counted was the weight of your missiles. In the Information Age, it is not the weight of missiles, but the speed of your Internet service. During the Cold War, there were two "superpowers," but in the Information Age no one is in control. During the Cold War, the formula was $E=MC^2$. In the Information Age, it is Moore's Law, which states that the power of processing doubles every 18 to 24 months. This law has been consistent for the last 30 years. During the Cold War, people counted on traditions. In the Information Age, people count on innovation.

During the Industrial Age, the two major economists were Karl Marx and John Maynard Keynes. During the Industrial Age, Marx and Keynes tried to control capitalism. However, the Information Age will batter and beat anybody who is thinking old Industrial Age ideas.

Our challenge is to evaluate our ideas and beliefs pertaining to money, employment, business, ministry, and investing. We cannot traverse a new landscape with old, worn-out maps. Today, one can be king of the hill one year, and at the bottom of the pile the next year. For people working for companies that do not change with the times, their entire business could be wiped away by the technological tidal wave that is sweeping across this world. Yesterday's children are now in jobs that were not even created when they were in school.

The Information Age requires "thinking" whereas the Industrial Age required "clinging." Many people make the mistake of "clinging" instead of "thinking." I worked with the same travel agent for roughly fifteen years. I used to tell her every few months that the Internet was going to radically change the travel industry. When she ran into some problems at work, instead of "thinking" about the future, she clung to the past. She eventually began to "think" and went to work for a more progressive travel agency. I changed agencies with her, and we work in a new travel paradigm today.

In the Industrial Age, the philosophy was to get a "safe, secure job." In the Information Age, the philosophy is "YOU, Inc.," where we work smart, and plan our own future. In the Industrial Age, a person stayed with one company. In the Information Age, the average person will work for and with as many as ten different companies. In the Industrial Age, we were taught never to make mistakes. In the Information Age, we have discovered that the answer is found in the problem.

We examine our calling, empower our commitments, explain our culture, and then equip our communication to provide a life-giving message to an audience within that culture. God-ordained preaching is designed to be interwoven both during the private phase of studying and the public phase of speaking the gospel. To fill the pulpit, the following precepts begin to help us build a theological and homiletical bridge between the purpose and preparations of communication. These precepts serve only as simple steps to the rest of the laws of communication.

The first precept of preaching is *scriptural*. Regardless of how dynamic a presentation is made by ministers, it will never be as effective as the Word of God. When we cause people to read the Word of God, the Word of God reads them. The Word of God is the power of God unto salvation (Rom 1:16), a source of faith (Rom 10:17), a hammer that breaks (Jer 23:29), and it is quick and powerful (Heb 4:12). God has promised to bless His Word (Isa 55:10-11), not the stories of the communicator. The old axiom goes, "God never puts a premium on an empty brain just because one has a full heart."

The second precept is *salvational*. Jesus Christ is the center of all good gospel preaching. Christ is the center of both the Old and New Testaments. Effective evangelistic preaching includes the doctrines of sin, the cross, the resurrection, judgment, the holiness of God, heaven, hell, repentance, faith, and Jesus Christ as Savior.

The third precept is *searching*. Preaching begins where people are and leads them to where they need to be. It does not condemn. It convicts the conscience, challenges the brain, and convinces the soul. It has been said, "You're never preaching until the audience hears another voice."

The fourth precept is *sensitive*. The presenter is to be positive and passionate. Every renowned preacher is not known only for handling the scripture, but for the deep communication of love for the listeners.

The fifth precept is *simple*. It is more difficult to put great truths into simple, everyday language than to use "Christianese." For people to respond to the gospel, we make it understandable. A message that is simple to comprehend is evidence of hard work and much study.

The sixth precept of preaching is *summons*. The invitation becomes the moral intersection where people will turn to Christ or take the wrong direction leading to hell. The invitation is a visual demonstration that God wants people to come to Him. The opportunity for people to confess Christ sends a signal from heaven that God accepts them as they are.

Throughout this entire book, we will focus repeatedly on the outcomes of our presentations. What is it we are hoping to achieve? Where will our people be in their thoughts when we finish speaking? Do we know how to prepare their hearts for the next presentation that we will give to them? We begin with the "end in mind" so we do not frustrate ourselves when our personal expectations are not met.

At the age of twelve, I came to Christ. It was July 15, 1973. I was called into fulltime ministry during the summer of 1975. I was eighteen years old when I began preaching weekends while attending the University of South Alabama, in Mobile, Alabama. In the mid-1990s, the Information Age flooded our world and a major chasm erupted between presenters and listeners. Before this *info-flood* each emerging generation has had its own ways of thinking about and viewing our world, but there is a greater misconnection today than in past generations.

You are now ready to begin one of the most exciting journeys today—to connect Gutenbergers and Googlers with the Gospel! How can we close the gap and connect at a higher level of impact? As we journey together we will learn that the left brain focuses on the *point of the passage* and the right brain focuses on the *picture for the presenter*. Whole brain presentations are a *package for the people*. While I was working through my graduate and doctoral studies, I quickly learned that the questions often being asked in the classroom are not the same questions being asked in the congregation.

We can be ministers who settle for preaching a sermon, but when we focus on the whole package, we can lift our ministry to a presentation of the sermon. We are going to look at the difference in preaching and a presentation of the Gospel.

Gutenbergers often lead from the *left* and the Googlers from the *right*. The left brain without the right is not delightful and right without the left not directed. Our overarching goal is to be able to bring the left and right together to produce and present dynamic presentations. Whether we are from the Gutenberg or Google tribe, let us remember that first and foremost we are called to "fill the pulpit and let God fill the building."

Left Brain
(Principles/Rational)

Right Brain
(Pictures/Relational)

LAW

2

PEOPLE BUY ON EMOTION
AND JUSTIFY WITH FACT

I make known to you, brethren, the gospel which
I preached to you, which also you received, in which also you stand,
by which also you are saved, if you hold fast the word which
I preached to you, unless you believed in vain. (1 Co 15:1-2)

On a sweltering July evening in a sports hall in Riga, Latvia, Bishop Kenneth C. Ulmer from Faithful Central Bible Church in Los Angeles, took the pulpit to address a jam-packed audience of first generation Christians who were scarcely a decade out of communist control. Through a Russian interpreter, Bishop Ulmer greeted the audience, then wound up a sermon that would eventually include walking the entire platform, acting out Bible characters, and having the audience repeat words back to him.

My wife, Sheri, and I had a front row seat for what could have been a Master Course in "Law Two." When I first read Burt Decker's statement, "People buy on emotion and justify with fact," it moved me to further study. Understanding this law is essential to close the gap between you and your audience and connect with them as quickly as possible, regardless of cultural, language, geographical, or generational gap. If we fail to connect on the emotional level, there will be little commitment to our presentation.

A year after that memorable evening, Bishop Ulmer brought his entire music team from Los Angeles to minister in Latvia again. He has preached and trained preachers on just about every continent, and succeeded Dr. Jack Hayford as President of Kings College and Seminary. For the last several years, Bishop Ulmer has graciously agreed to close the pastors conferences that I have facilitated, bringing the flow of presentations to a final crescendo and drawing ministers and church members alike from all Christian streams to personal altars of recommitment and rededication to the Gospel.

Certain communication laws empower the presenters with the ability to impact and influence their audience in captivating and memorable ways. Making the leap from the Gutenberg to the Google world is easier once we understand how people think, regardless of the cultural context. The presentation style of Jesus Christ illustrates His understanding of how His audience thought and how they applied truth to their lives.

We can examine exegetically the speeches and sermons of the New Testament and ask a variety of questions relating to evangelistic preaching. Who was the finest preacher in the New Testament? Who "connected" and "communicated" with his audience more effectively than any other New Testament evangelist? Was it the Seventy? Was it Philip? Paul? Or was it Jesus?

Jesus Christ served as a Spirit-filled preacher in the New Testament era. Even though one could argue that John the Baptist served as an evangelist in the New Testament era, Jesus ascribed John as the greatest of all the "prophets" (Mt 11:7-15; Lk 7:26-28). Jesus followed the two-fold ministry tracks of evangelizing the lost and equipping the saints (Eph 4:11-16). Christ trained leaders for the purpose of evangelism. He was the great physician, the master teacher, the suffering servant, and He was the excellent evangelist. He epitomizes the "preacher's paradigm" for culturally relevant, Bible-based, Spirit-empowered evangelistic preaching that produces changed lives.

Jesus was a master communicator. He inductively and deductively combined "the text" with His "times" for the dual purposes of evangelizing the lost and equipping His disciples. To be more effective in the twenty-first century, we need to compare and contrast our preaching ministry to the first-century evangelistic preaching ministry of Jesus. In this digital world we have to be able to combine principle and picture together to connect with this visual world.

It is possible to study the spirit, substance, and style of the dynamic preaching of Jesus. Twenty percent of the New Testament is comprised of the actual words of Christ. The total recorded words of Jesus is the "approximate equivalent of ten thirty-minute sermons" (Ralph Lewis, 13).

PREACH A COMMUNICATED GOSPEL

We must preach to communicate the gospel. Teaching is not simply talking. Learning is not simply listening. What does it mean to communicate? The term "communication" comes from the Latin word *communis*, meaning "common." Commonness or commonality must first be established before effective communication can take place between people (Hendricks 1987, 98). The more the communicator builds a commonality between the message and the listeners, the higher the level of communication between presenter and the audience. It is the responsibility of the presenter to make sure the audience understands and applies the message to their lives. "True biblical teaching doesn't take place unless the students have learned." (Wilkinson, 26-27) What does it mean to "teach" and "to learn"? Are these concepts related?

When Moses spoke to his people in Deuteronomy, he used the word "teach" (4:1) and "learn" (5:1) in his message. In the Hebrew, the term is the same for "teach" as for "learn." He did not separate teaching and learning. How can ministers know if we are effectively communicating the gospel? We can know by what the audience learns and applies to their lives. (Wilkinson, 26-27)

There must be a balance between beginning with the needs of the people or the precepts of Scripture. On the one hand, people determine the starting point of the sermon. On the other hand, the Scripture determines the subject and substance of the sermon. We do not abdicate the supremacy of Scripture or the biblical basis for the sermon. We simply recognize the simple truth that preachers must begin where people are and not expect them to come up first to the preacher's level.

In John 4, we read that Jesus went to Samaria to preach the gospel. Jesus' conversation with the woman at the well is an excellent model for ministers who wish to communicate the gospel effectively. Jesus came into this world "to seek and to save that which was lost" (Lk 19:10). Just as Jesus could not reach the Samaritans by preaching the gospel in Jerusalem, ministers cannot preach evangelistically unless we are committed to "communicating" the gospel. According to author Ron Hutchcraft, ministers must be willing to communicate the gospel "on their turf"..."in their people group"...and "in their language." Evangelistic preaching requires the preachers to speak in a language that can be understood. Ministers "have to translate the Gospel, not just transmit it" (Hutchcraft, 59). Translation is difficult in a constantly changing culture. "Christianese" is a foreign language in a post-Christian culture.

PREACH A CONNECTED GOSPEL

The preacher must have a point of contact with the audience. If there is no contact during the sermon, there most likely will be no response to the invitation. The point of contact for Jesus with the woman at the well in Samaria was, "Give Me a drink" (Jn 4:7). He began with the physical thirst before moving to spiritual thirst (Hutchcraft, 60). What are the points of contact for preachers today?

Jesus engaged His listeners. He used stories, dialogue, questions, comparisons and contrasts, common experiences, creativity, metaphors, and imagination to connect the gospel to His generation. Jesus went from the concrete to the abstract, from the facts to the principles, from the data to the dictum.

The preaching of Jesus scratched where people itched in everyday life. Ralph and Gregg Lewis have provided a list of Jesus' preaching topics. Jesus spoke on:

> Adultery, anger, anxiety, avarice, death, debts, doubts, eternity, faith, fasting, fault-finding, giving, greed, honesty, hypocrisy, joy, kindness, knowledge, law, legalism, life, lust, marriage, money, oaths, parenthood, prayer, pretense, respect, responsibility, reward, rulers, sex, slander, speech, stewardship, taxes, trust, unkindness, virtue, wisdom, and zeal. (Ralph Lewis, 29)

Technology may change, but the needs of people remain basically the same. Every topic in the list above is still a contemporary need in our society. Jesus knew how to connect with His listeners.

Jesus connected with His hearers by stories, parables, illustrations. Everyone loves a good story. According to Mark 4:34, "He did not speak to them without a parable." A descriptive story turns ears into eyes so people can see the "truth" in everyday life. Thirty-three percent of all the recorded teachings of Christ were parables or stories. However, sermonizers cannot simply make contemporary stories the basis of their sermons. *Stories move people, but the Word of God changes people.*

We must learn how to release the power of the inner brain and become more relaxed, confident, and informal in our communicating and more persuasive at reaching the inner brain of our listeners. The outer brain is located right between our ears. Robert Jastrow observed in *The Enchanted Loom,* "The human brain is more complicated than the astronomer's universe. It is the most complicated object that science has ever tried to understand."

The whole brain contains nearly ten billion nerve cells. Because of the intricate complexity of the brain's circuitry, the number of possible interconnec-

Stories move people, but the Word of God changes people.

tions between the cells of our brain is many orders of magnitude greater than the number of atoms in the entire universe. That is amazing! The vast elaborate circuitry of the human brain gives it a subtlety and speed that even a hundred crazed super computers working in sync could never hope to match. Mind researchers believe the human brain is capable of reviewing up to 10,000 separate factors at once. The possible number of connections in the universe is one followed by a hundred zeros, but the number of different interconnections possible in the human brain is one followed by eight hundred zeros. (Decker, 256-257)

For culturally-relevant ministers to persuade their listeners to believe the gospel, they must not only build a bridge between the spiritual and the physical but also between the spiritual and mental. Learning involves the inner and outer brain which has a dual nature. In the outer brain are two halves. "The left side deals more with facts, the right side more

communication must pass. The gate is attended by a gatekeeper, standing guard at the house of the intellect. Our gatekeeper is the "inner brain."

The inner brain is our emotional brain. The inner brain physically directs our outer brain or our "thinking" brain. The inner brain makes us cringe at an explosion. It is our survival mechanism. It makes us jump back from something that is too hot. It signals us when it is time to eat or drink. The inner brain is the emotional part of the brain. The inner brain makes the decision whether a person is believable or trustworthy. The outer "thinking" brain is where language is developed. This is where creativity and decision-making take place (Decker, 69).

The inner brain answers one question: *"Is this information safe?"* If we are energetic, enthusiastic, and believable, our words may make it to the outer brain. If we are nervous and boring, then our words will never have impact. The message will be tuned out.

This has to do with how we present before a congregation. If we plan to communicate with our listeners, we must make an emotional connection so the inner brain will pass on the information to the thinking brain. The gatekeeper has sole control. Will the gatekeeper open the gate of communication? Will the message get through, or will it be blocked? When we understand how the brain works, we are then be able to use the entire brain when speaking.

PREACH A CONTINUED GOSPEL

We make the emotional connection at the beginning, maintain interest, and end with a bang. The stories of our lives are among the best tools in our tool kit. The use of images and metaphors, whether created by language or by visual support, helps us keep the connection to people.

Why do our listeners need help in listening and remembering? Because our audience has a chronic case of information overload. The average attention span of an adult is only eight minutes. For children, the attention span is only six minutes. The mind loves images and emotional stimuli. Images are vital because of the makeup of our first and second brains:

1. **Within our first brain is a component called the hippocampus.** The hippocampus is triggered by feelings of sorrow, joy, or fear. When

the hippocampus comes in contact with things that trigger this response, it records the impression as a DVD records a video. The record button is pushed, and the image is stored in the long-term memory portion of the brain. This is why we remember so vividly the birth of a child, the explosion of the Challenger, the fall of the Twin Towers (Decker, 282-285)

2. **It is the speaker's responsibility to discover what appropriate images or memory hooks are necessary in a presentation.** Make your presentations SHARP:

- Stories
- Humor
- Analogies
- References and quotes
- Pictures and visual aids

All of the SHARP principles have one thing in common. They all work together to bring life to your presentation. They all engage the listener to see and feel the presentation in their minds or on the emotional level. You must add SHARPs to make the sermon memorable.

Stories and examples: Long before there was writing, there were stories. The art form of passing stories from generation to generation has been neglected. The key to a good story is the ability to tap into the heart. A good story moves us from thinking to feeling. A good story takes us to that place in time.

Tips:

Be brief.

Use sensory language.

Be conversational.

After the story, state your point explicitly and link it back to the main theme. Make them like Velcro—stories that stick to the heart.

Humor: This is not about telling jokes. This is the concept of adding lightness and personality to yourself and your presentation. Humor is more humanization. It builds a bond between you and the audience.

Tips:

> Lighten up on your attitude about how you think about yourself.
>
> Do not expect belly laughs.
>
> Smile and allow time for humor to have its effect.
>
> Exaggerate certain portions of your content to reach humorous proportions.

Analogies: It is a natural function of the mind to compare, contrast, categorize, and cross-reference. That is what creates analogies. Ask yourself in advance how a concept or idea is like something else. Appropriate analogies make the complex simple and not the simple complex.

References and quotes: This is independent information cited to support your point of view or main thrust of a certain part of your presentation. This information can come from newspapers, magazines, books, interviews, tapes, etc. Quotes can be formal or restated to make them more memorable. Quotes add depth to your presentation.

Tips:

> Read a quote rather than misquoting what someone once said.
>
> Be sure to acknowledge the source.
>
> Introduce the reference or quote to cause your listener to pay careful attention to what is about to be said and heard.
>
> Select only the powerful portions. Do not make the quote too long.

Pictures and Visual Aids: People basically remember two things more than anything else when a presentation is completed: the emotional tone of the speaker and the visual images of the speaker and the visual aids. When an audience sees as well as hears a presentation, retention increases from 14 percent to 38 percent. Speakers' goals are met 34 percent of the time when visuals are used during the communication. Group consensus is 21 percent higher in meetings at which visual aids are incorporated. The time required to communicate a concept can be reduced up to 40 percent with the use of visuals. But remember, visuals are supports, not the message. We will talk more about them later. Visuals awaken the first brain. They increase the listener's attention span.

Tips:

Use color: It attracts attention and increases retention as much as three or four times. Select your background colors first and then select your script color. Make it easy on the eyes.

Simple to read and easy to absorb: Use the one-concept-per-visual rule. This will allow the audience time to digest the concept in eight minutes. Do not put a lot of text on each slide. Say more than you show. Do not show more than you say. Use conceptual visuals to make the point. When you use text, do not read it. Your audience can read it for themselves. Stand a body length from your computer and see if you can easily read your slide. Or, lay an overhead on the floor, stand over it, and see if you can read it. If you cannot read it, then the wording is too small for the audience.

Keep the visuals balanced to make them proportionate and organized. Make them fit natural tendencies.

Variety is the spice of life. In other words, use graphics, pie charts, photos, and video clips.

In composition, use contrasting colors, bullets, italics, and larger fonts to focus your audience on the key elements. Fancy type slows the reader down. Make charts match what you are trying to say. Good charts are immediately comprehended. Let the visuals give the point of view of what the numbers mean. Save the details for a handout.

I challenge you spend some time thinking about some of your biggest decisions in life. I believe you will find when you made your final decision that you first connected at the emotional level followed by facts to justify or solidify your decision in each instance. It is imperative that during our presentations that we connect emotionally with our listeners if we desire for our messages to have lasting impact.

Left Brain

(Principles/Rational)

Right Brain

(Pictures/Relational)

LAW

3

BEGIN WITH THE END IN MIND

Do the work of an evangelist, fulfill your ministry. (2 Tim 4:5)

"Just as I am...." The words alone bring to mind the familiar tune that is a staple of commitment times and altar calls. The song brings to mind images as well. One image seared in the minds of thousands of Christians over the last decades has been the meetings held by the great evangelist Billy Graham. The Billy Graham Evangelistic Association is now airing on television many of the evangelist's past "crusades." In a bygone era, these were the biggest and most newsworthy happenings in a city. They emptied office buildings and stopped traffic. At the end of the sermon, people streamed to the front by the thousands to the words of this song.

Dr. Billy Graham served as the Honorary Chairman on two Executive Planning Committees on which I was privileged to serve for the 1994 "North American Conference of Itinerant Evangelists" and "Amsterdam 2000." During planning sessions, it was clear that Dr. Graham consistently had the end in mind. He would always challenge us to focus on the salvation of the lost and fulfillment of the Great Commission.

Should you be privileged to view one of his masterful messages, I recommend that you overlook the black and white images, crisp bow ties, saddle shoes and dirndl dresses. If you have the opportunity to witness the great Billy Graham calling people to Christ, get out your pencil to take notes, study it hard, review it often, and learn from a master of the invitation.

There is a fundamental difference in aim between a lecturer and a biblical preacher. A lecturer explains a subject. A biblical preacher seeks character change in the hearts and lives of the listeners. A lecturer explains botany. A preacher raises flowers. The minister is called to present the gospel in such a manner that lives are forever changed.

The goal of a message is to persuade people. The basic components are: interpretation, application, and then invitation. The main purpose of a sermon is not simply to exegete a text correctly but also to produce godly character in people's lives. We must begin with the correct end in mind. As a result of the sermon, the congregation should live out the principles that were proposed in the message.

The purpose of our public preaching is fueled by our private philosophies of ministry. Contemplate the following questions. They are designed to challenge you to evaluate what forces have shaped you and determined how your life has turned out up to now. Have you ever stopped to think about the kind of life you are living—and more importantly, why? For example, why do you live where you live? Why are you involved in your present kind of ministry? Why do you preach the way you preach? Why are you a pastor, missionary, or evangelist? What about your family and friends? What are they like?

It is important to look at the "whys" of life. When we are able to answer the "whys," we are able to determine the starting point of a more productive and fruitful future. To begin a journey to a new location, we must know the starting point. We have to know where we are in order to know how to get where we want to go. Your audience is the same way. It doesn't start with them. It starts inside the minister's heart. The principle is: You have to answer "Why" before you can get to "Wow."

The philosopher George Santayana observed, "The loftiest edifices need the deepest foundations." This metaphor applies to our lives and our ministries. The problem today is that a lot of people are all house and no foundation. The stronger our foundation, the easier it is to build an enduring ministry.

We cannot teach what we do not know, cannot give what we do not have and cannot lead others where we have not been. Once we have a rock-solid biblical philosophy regarding life and ministry, we will be able to live out "the changed life."

What constitutes the foundation of our life and ministry? What single concept influences our overall life? The word is "philosophy." Our philosophy of life and ministry is the foundation of who we are. It is the cornerstone for our behavior, our daily habits, our relationships with others, and our future. Our philosophy of ministry ultimately determines what we will achieve in the harvest field.

The dictionary defines philosophy as "a system of values by which one lives." It is our belief system. It is a paradigm or filter that is used to view our outside world. Our philosophy is the "master operation system" that guides our lives. What is your philosophy about God and eternity? Does the way you live reflect this philosophy, or are your habits in life really portraying a different philosophy?

Have you ever thought through your philosophy of ministry? If so, what is it? What are your core beliefs in your preaching ministry? Are you practicing your core beliefs? Are you living according to your philosophy of ministry?

Think about all of these ideas for a moment. What you believe creates who you are in your family, ministry, and community. We interpret the world based upon what we believe to be true. Our conclusions about ourselves and others are based upon what we believe about ourselves and what we believe others to be as well. What is your philosophy concerning money, marriage, health, the Church, the world, and the future? Even if you have not carefully written down your philosophy concerning these areas, you still have core beliefs relating to them.

In this section, our goal is to be able to flesh out our philosophy of ministry so we can cognitively makes decisions in the future that fully reflect our belief system. Let's decide what we believe and do not believe about preaching and the proclamation of the gospel. Each of us has a philosophy of life and ministry even though we may not take the time to articulate it. If our philosophy of ministry does not reflect our personal goals or aspirations, then we will never reach those goals. We need to review and rethink our philosophy to create a more dynamic ministry.

Once you have carefully evaluated the kind of philosophy of ministry and preaching you presently have, ask yourself: "Where is my philosophy of ministry taking me? What effects will my current beliefs have on my ministry in the next five years?" If you conclude that you need to make changes, here are some simple steps to update your philosophy:

1. Clean out your old closet of beliefs. Keep what is biblical and practical. Throw the rest away. Ask yourself: Are my present beliefs hurting or helping me?
2. Create a list of core beliefs pertaining to your preaching ministry. What are the non-negotiables? How important is preaching to you?
3. Compare your updated core beliefs to your present preaching ministry.
4. Commit to making the necessary changes in your weekly schedule and ministry to genuinely reflect your philosophy of ministry.

Over the years as I have traveled, I have carefully observed the libraries of pastors. On one occasion, as a pastor and I were chatting before the Sunday morning service began, I asked him to recommend a good book for me to read in the near future. The pastor responded, "I have not read a new book in seven years. The preacher does not need to read a lot in order to faithfully preach the gospel. I believe that the Lord will pour a message into my life just prior to the Sunday services."

What would you say are the core values of this pastor as they relate to the preaching of the gospel?

On another occasion, I was privileged to minister for a week with a leading pastor in North America. During the week, we spoke of our views on preaching, evangelism, and discipleship. This well-organized pastor told me he has a preaching calendar that contains all the messages he plans to preach throughout the year. He believes that half the battle for the local pastor is deciding what to preach each week to his or her congregation. He also believes the Holy Spirit will anoint the study time of the pastor just as much as the preaching time during the service.

What would you say are the core values of this pastor as they relate to the preaching of the gospel?

A lot of ministers are "two hours ahead of the hounds." They are on the run, endeavoring to get ready because "Sunday's comin'." With a solid philosophy and planning, the minister will find far greater enjoyment in preaching the gospel and providing a life-changing bridge from the past life to eternal life. When communicating to both Gutenbergers and Googlers, we need to think about the end in mind. What are we trying to accomplish? What are the outcomes we hope to achieve?

If the target cannot be seen, our thinking will be fuzzy throughout our development and delivery of the message. While I am preparing a message, regardless of the age of the audience, I am fine-tuning the end in mind and what kind of invitation I will give after the message. If there is an uncertain sound in my voice or a hesitancy in my actions, the invitation will not be perceived as authoritative.

Our philosophy of preaching determines how we view our role as a preacher, how we schedule time for our preparation, what books we read, how we deliver the message, and the results we believe that will be achieved. As ministers, we must think with the end in mind. The most effective preachers start with the invitation to Christ at the beginning of sermon preparation, not the end. We view the end from the beginning. Life-changing invitations do not just happen at the close of evangelistic messages. Billy Graham provides classic examples of starting the invitation from the beginning. From the basic components of interpretation, application and invitation, we start with the end in mind, the invitation. What do we want people to do about what we say?

THE PURPOSE OF THE INVITATION

The invitation brings into focus the answer to the question: *What do I want to accomplish by delivering this message?* This is the objective actualized. When a communicator has accomplished the objective, he or she can shout, "Bull's eye!" Regardless of the kind of presentation that you bring, some creative response or invitation is given to the audience. As you prepare your message, if thoughts, words, and actions do not support your objective, your main thrust of the sermon, do not include them. Regardless of how great they sound over coffee with a friend, hold them for another day. *Only include what supports your objective.*

The invitation causes the audience to make a decision regarding the objective. By the conclusion of the impartation and invitation, people will _____. It is the presenter's responsibility to fill in the blank. As a result of hearing a message, people will be able to understand something or be able to do something.

What is an invitation? Street defines it as follows:

> The invitation is that act by which the preacher of the gospel exhorts his hearers and instructs them how to appropriate the content of the *kerygma* [gospel] in their individual lives. Any sermon that does not include an invitation as well as a proclamation is not New Testament-style preaching. Every sermon should aim to stir the human will. Truth is something that must be obeyed. It is the gospel invitation that presses home the claims of Christ and calls for an immediate response. (Street, 37)

Just as the first century messenger concluded the message with an invitation for people to repent of sin and place their faith in the Lord Jesus Christ for salvation, the twenty-first century communicator should strive to invite people to come to Christ for eternal life.

THE PRIORITY OF THE INVITATION

Most ministers I have met over the years struggle with the development and delivery of an effective invitation. When we try to find reading or video resources to help, there is not a great amount of help available to us.

The invitation is the logical climax of the message. Without it, the message is incomplete and its effects unknown. Every evangelistic sermon succeeds or fails according to the effectiveness of the invitation. The main goal of the gospel is to bring men and women into a saving relationship with Jesus Christ. Preaching has no more important function than the issuing of an effective invitation. Most ministers do not know how to issue a good, persuasive invitation.

THE PRESUPPOSITIONS OF THE INVITATION

Why should a minister give a public invitation? There are many church fellowships and even seminaries that teach against an active invitation or simply do not include one, perhaps for traditional reasons. Here are just six reasons that the invitation is crucial for every sermon:

1. *The invitation is biblical.* The Old and New Testaments are filled with invitations from God, Christ, the prophets, apostles, and evangelists.

2. *Invitations are psychological.* Emotions aroused and desires stirred will soon pass away unless acted upon at once. Good impulses are harder to generate the second time than they were the first time if the first impulse did not result in action. This is why some lost people say church simply "inoculated" them from the Gospel message. We need not wait another day that could lull them into inaction. We act when their hearts are open and they are ready (Whitesell, 11-21)

3. *The invitation is historical.* Church history is filled with examples of the effectiveness of the public invitation. Famous evangelists in the annals of Church history were masters at giving persuasive, public invitations.

4. *Invitations are salvational.* They aid in bringing people to Jesus Christ.

5. *Invitations are logical.* If ministers are willing to instruct people regarding the salvation of their souls, then they should logically extend an invitation to experience forgiveness of sin immediately.

6. *Invitations are spiritual.* They are spiritual both for the preacher and the audience. The minister must depend upon the convicting presence of the Holy Spirit, and the lost must express their spiritual need of Christ (Street, 139-146).

THE PHASES OF THE INVITATION

Praying

Set time aside for preparing your invitation. God will provide help and guidance. Pray specifically for every aspect of the invitation and especially for yourself, that God will break your heart concerning the lost condition of many in your services. It has been said that preaching could be spelled "pre-aching." The preacher without an ache in his or her heart will be unable to move the audience.

By communing with Christ in prayer, the concern the Lord has for the souls of men and women becomes our concern. When we reach that point, much of the battle has been won. The great orator Charles Spurgeon said, "A burning heart will soon find for itself a flaming tongue."

Persuading

"It is not enough to instruct the lost and warn them of impending doom, they must be persuaded" (Autrey, 127). J. I. Packer wrote,

Evangelizing, therefore, is not simply a matter of teaching, and instructing, and imparting information to the mind. There is more to it than that. Evangelizing includes the endeavor to elicit a response to the truth taught. It is communication with a view to conversion. It is a matter, not merely of informing, but also of inviting. It is an attempt to *gain*, or *win*, or *catch*, our fellow-men for Christ.

Be certain your invitation seeks to move the will of your hearers, to bring their will into submission to the person of Jesus Christ. Your main goal is to obtain a favorable verdict immediately, calling each individual in your audience to embrace the truth of the gospel and yield to Christ as Lord and Savior. Let it be said of your preaching that the only reason people remain lost once presented with the Good News is because of willful disobedience. "Almost persuaded" doomed King Agrippa when he refused to respond to the Apostle Paul's invitation (Acts 26:28).

There are two avenues of approaching the will: the intellect and the emotions. A person can be moved to action if the mind can be convinced the action is necessary. Bring your listener to the point where he or she says, "I can be saved (mind). I must be saved (emotions). I will be saved (will)."

To achieve this result, first there needs to be logic in the presentation of the gospel. Next, the communicator must take aim at the heart. Intellectual acceptance of the facts alone does not save. Men and women must be moved to take action. This is accomplished by speaking to their consciences. Logic has its place, but it must be set ablaze. Spurgeon advises: "A sinner has a heart as well as a head; a sinner has emotions as well as thoughts; and we must appeal to both. A sinner will never be converted until his emotions are stirred. Unless he feels sorrow for sin." (Spurgeon, 1963, 26)

How does a minister prepare and give an effective public invitation? In order for an invitation to be persuasive, it must "be tied in closely with the major thrust of the sermon…. In other words, it should grow out of the main theme of the message so that the people will not be surprised when it is given." (Perry, 113) It should also be implicit throughout the sermon to prepare people for their response. Remember, the effective minister looks for ways to imply the invitation throughout the entire development of the evangelistic message. Much practice comes before the presentation of powerful invitations.

What characterizes an effective invitation? In order to prepare and deliver an effective invitation, the preacher must pray, use appropriate transitions leading into the invitation and away from the main body of the sermon, ethically persuade people, extend a public call, and be led by the Holy Spirit.

When should the minister issue an invitation? The "natural" response to this question is at the end of the message. However, the "supernatural" response is when the Holy Spirit wants the minister to begin and conclude the invitation. Timing is crucial to presenting an effective, life-changing invitation to people. However, the evangelist or pastor must not forget to allow enough time for the invitation to be issued and for the Holy Spirit to work in the hearts of the lost.

The late Edwin Louis Cole routinely gave the altar call first in the men's meetings he held around the world. He would simply lead the entire crowd in a confession of Christ then say, "You know why you are here, so don't sit there feeling guilty. If this is your first time to confess Christ publicly, come forward so we can pray a prayer of confirmation over you." He became a master at seizing the moment and simply called for a response from the audience anytime through his message. After the response, he continued on with the message to the end. This unusual approach is powerfully effective. Some ministers become masters at seizing the moment.

Planning

The preacher must plan to issue an effective call for people to act upon the truth. If we fail here, the rest of the presentation is useless. The mark of a successful invitation is people persuaded to come to Christ.

Emotions can be aroused and the intellect stirred, but unless the lost are challenged to exercise their will and given opportunity to do so, it is unlikely they will do it on their own. This is why the public invitation is the hub of the evangelistic sermon.

Make the content simple. Prepare the content of your appeal. For example:

> "As _____ begins to sing in just a moment, I am going to ask you to step to the nearest aisle. Every aisle leads to the front of this platform. I will be standing here, on the main floor, waiting for you to arrive. If you do not desire to come alone, ask someone around you to walk with you.

> Jesus Christ called for a public confession of His disciples. I am asking you to follow the commands of Christ and come forward now." (This could be to another prearranged location. More options are listed in the next section.).

Make the invitation personal.

> "Regardless of your position in life, you need to come. Regardless of what you have done in life, you need to come now. Regardless of your background, please do not procrastinate. You need to come. I am waiting on you."

Make the invitation positive.

Do not issue an apology. You not only have the right to issue the call but also a divine obligation. Once again, Charles Spurgeon hit a home run on this: "Ambassadors do not apologize when they go to a foreign court; they know that their monarch has sent them, and they deliver their message with all the authority of king and country at their back." (Spurgeon, 1963, 84)

> "God has spoken to you tonight. There will never be a better opportunity to have your sins forgiven than tonight. Tomorrow you will have less time than today. Tomorrow you will have more sin and less time to get right with God. Tomorrow you will have a harder heart because of more sin and less time to obtain forgiveness.

Furthermore, God may never call you to repentance again. Come now. I am waiting for you."

Time is a vital consideration. The general rule of thumb is "the shorter, the better." Also, you should be able to deliver your invitation without notes. Eye contact is extremely important.

Patience

Another general rule is to wait patiently for people to respond after the final call has been given. At this juncture, you must turn the results over to the Holy Spirit. Resist the temptation to coax, to make numerous additional exhortations, or even to manipulate people into taking action. These pressure tactics are often used by ministers who are afraid no one will respond to their invitation. A fear of embarrassment and failure has caused many otherwise honest preachers to use trickery in obtaining results. Exercise each of these phases to see better results.

THE PRACTICS OF THE INVITATION

Invitations are divided into two major categories: those which call upon people to make an immediate decision for Christ or the issues raised in the message and those which call for a delayed response.

The Delayed-Response Invitation

The delayed-response invitation challenges listeners to ponder the content of the gospel and then decide if they desire to become a Christian or respond to another need that surfaced during the message. If the decision is positive, they can arrange to meet the pastor or evangelist at a designated time and location.

The After-Meeting: The after-meeting takes place 10 or 15 minutes after the close of the worship or evangelistic service. At the end of the sermon, the preacher invites those in the audience who are interested in becoming Christians to meet in another room. In this meeting, any questions are answered, prayer is offered, and these individuals are led in becoming believers in Christ.

There are advantages to the after-meeting.
1. Eliminates undue pressure.
2. Eliminates embarrassment.
3. Eliminates the dramatic element.
4. Separates the sincere seekers from the curiosity seekers.

Special Appointments: The minister invites those who are interested in becoming Christians to contact the church office and to set up a private meeting.

Signing of Cards: Some ministers are more comfortable in having inquirers' cards placed in each pew or chair. Those who are desirous of additional information about their salvation are urged at the close of the gospel message to fill in the card including name, address, and telephone number. The card is given to an usher or the pastor at the end of the service or is left on the seat.

Drawbacks: There are some drawbacks to this method, which you should make yourself fully aware of before you choose it:
1. The most serious defect of a delayed-response invitation is that God calls sinners to be saved immediately, not 15 minutes later, not 3 days later, or 1 week later (2 Co 6:2; Mt 4:17; Mk 1:16-20; Mt 8:21-22).
2. A delayed-response also allows the convicted person an opportunity to slip out the back door and quench the voice of the Holy Spirit. The Spirit of God speaks through the Word of God to produce faith and draw men to Christ. People are more likely to receive Christ when under conviction.
3. The delayed-response invitation gives Satan an opportunity to snatch away the Word that has been placed in the sinner's heart (Lk 8:5, 11, 12).
4. Waiting to deal with a person about salvation begs the question if the Heavenly Father may not draw the person at a later date (Jn 6:44) (Street, 169-76).

The Immediate-Response Invitation

Any invitation that calls upon unbelievers to repent and trust Christ, then gives an immediate opportunity to do so is an immediate-response invitation.

Raising of Hands: Ask for a showing of hands of those who desire to accept Christ in their lives.

    a. Tell them to meet with an usher after the service.

    b. Tell them ushers will be walking down the aisles to accept the response cards.

    c. Ask them to come forward to accept Christ.

Standing for Salvation: At the close of the invitation, ask those who desire to give their lives to Christ to stand. You could ask the friend who brought them, or someone sitting near them to stand with them. One way to lead up to your invitation is simply to ask for a show of hands of those who were saved in their childhood, teens, 20s, 30s and so on. This illustrates that the longer one waits, the less likelihood he or she will accept Christ.

Praying in Private: At the close of the invitation, invite members of the audience to close their eyes and ask those who are dedicating their lives to Christ to pray quietly at their seats while the worship leader leads a chorus of worship.

Verbal Confessions: At close of the invitation, the minister leads the entire congregation in the sinner's prayer and confession of Christ. After the time of prayer and confession, ask for a show of hands of those who made first-time decisions to become followers of Christ.

Coming Forward: Most invitations include the request to come to the front of the sanctuary. We have the right to expect this of people whom the Holy Spirit is convicting. At this point, the preacher should come down from the platform and stand level with the front row of chairs or pews. Here are some ways to invite people to come forward:

1. Extend an invitation and have the altar workers lead the way.
2. Extend an invitation and have the entire congregation come forward and lead the lost in prayer and confession.
3. Extend an invitation from a baptistery.
4. Extend an invitation at the end of communion.
5. Extend a funeral service invitation.
6. Extend an invitation and then have the lost come forward. As the lost come forward, have the altar workers join them in the aisles.
7. Extend an invitation and ask for a show of hands. While their hands are raised, ask them to come forward.

One of the greatest tragedies is the person leaving the service with the intention of accepting Christ but not being given the opportunity to do so. Every minister wants to see the product of his or her investment into the lives of others (Street, 177-185).

Meng-Tse, a Chinese philosopher who lived more than 2,000 years ago, said: "To act without clear understanding, to form habits without investigation, to follow a path all one's life without knowing where it really leads—such is the behavior of the multitude." Solomon wrote: "They made me caretaker of the vineyards, but I have not taken care of my own vineyard" (Song 1:6). In other words, we must make certain our philosophy of life and ministry are reflected in the vineyard God has given us to oversee, organize, and overcome.

What is your vineyard? Are you living your life or someone else's life? A well-balanced philosophy of ministry in particular and a well-rounded philosophy of life in general will govern and guide our lives in the future. The purpose of each and every one of your presentations is to produce godly character in people's lives.

Left Brain
(Principles/Rational)

Right Brain
(Pictures/Relational)

LAW

---------------- 4 ----------------

CREATIVE PRESENTATIONS ARE LIKE GIVING BIRTH TO BARBWIRE BUT SOMEONE HAS TO DO IT

The time will come when they will not endure sound doctrine but wanting to have their ears tickled, they will accumulate for themselves teachers in accordance to their own desires, and will turn away their ears from the truth and will turn aside to myths. (2 Tim 2:3-4)

In the spring of 2009, I attended graduation ceremonies at a renowned seminary in the United States to witness an earned doctorate conferred on a friend's son. The commencement speaker was a Professor of Preaching from another well-known seminary. For the graduation of these fine scholars, culminating years of schooling, the educator gave the most embarrassing "Gospel presentation" I have ever heard. And I have heard a lot!

To begin his talk, the professor made condescending references to the faculty behind him and told the graduating class that they would never remember anything about his message. He proceeded to speak without taking a biblical text, nor would he quote a single Scripture over the next forty minutes. He announced his title was "Three Bs" but he did not connect the "Three Bs" to anything, like the "Three Bs of Ministry."

This presenter launched into commentary on American history, evidently not considering that fully 30 percent of the class were students from outside the US. My friend was from India. The presenter cast one of America's Founding Fathers in a negative light and contrasted him to a well-known contemporary. The US students would know that both men were famously guilty of adultery, but the presenter described the Founding Father as a disgusting leader and the contemporary leader as an angel. No Scripture was provided to bring balance, clarity, or even to attempt to prove his shaky premise.

If I had been surprised by what I heard at the start, it paled in comparison to his shocking conclusions. For his last point, his "B" stood for a bodily function which led him for ten minutes to read a children's fable in order to point out how one can become an agent of change. The man's lack of biblical communication and failure to recognize the DNA of his audience was all the more embarrassing because of sharing it with my distinguished friend whose son had worked hard, despite a transcontinental commute, to earn his doctorate. I trust that educator will be proved wrong and his words will be memorialized for years, as that group of graduates does the exact opposite of his example.

This was one presentation, but I have noticed a trend among preachers who recognize the chasm of communication that has widened enormously over the last two decades. They realize that "common knowledge" about the Bible in this culture does not exist anymore. Added to this obvious misconnect, they perceive with stark clarity that the information explosion has given Googlers a different worldview and driven them even further from any Gospel understanding. Yet, the trend I have seen is for ministers to resort to shameful tricks and techniques to grab the attention of the Googlers, even if at the expense of the Gutenbergers, the Gospel, and good manners.

It is true that whether we were born among the Googlers or the Gutenbergers, we have to move from misconnection and miscommunication to influence and impact in the hearts of our listeners. Of course, the closer we are to an age group, the faster it is to cross the chasm of communication to that group. But, if anyone ever told you preparing powerful presentations is easy, then he or she does not comprehend contemporary obstacles that communicators face today.

Growth is what success is all about. Change is inevitable, but growth is optional. We have to be willing to change in our rapidly-changing world where the attention spans of most people are shrinking and the power of concentration has been devalued.

The age of rhetoric is dead. Too many speech teachers describe speaking as a medium of words rather than a medium of sight and sound which happens to use words. Reading speeches will not work.

God created us to understand truth through pictures painted in our minds. From Genesis to Revelation, God's Word is filled with the "pictures of God" that communicate to His world. When Jesus was born in Bethlehem, He came to us as the outward expression of the inward thoughts of God. He is the "picture" of the essence of Who the Father is. Jesus said, "If you have SEEN ME you have SEEN the Father."

Complications for Your Audience

Though it may be hard to develop and deliver creative, compelling messages with the right process in place, we *will* improve. As we go through this book, we will cover in detail the top mistakes in communicating today. In summary, they are:

1. *Allowing fear to block you.* Forty-one percent of people fear public speaking more than anything else in life while only seven percent of people fear death. Learn to recognize the levels and signs of fear:

> *Too many speech teachers describe speaking as a medium of words rather than a medium of sight and sound which happens to use words.*

(1) Terror—The extreme. Usually the person just does not feel adequate.

(2) Fear—The person feels somewhat adequate but does not enjoy speaking. He or she would rather be spoken to rather than be the speaker.

(3) Heightened tension—The person does it but does not enjoy speaking.

(4) Stimulation—The person does not flee but flies. He or she is able to connect with people. Leaders are in this level. They have turned harmful stress into helpful power.

You can move through these levels of fear and overcome them by keeping this checklist as a point of reference before you enter any platform:

(1) Know your material cold.

(2) Know yourself and how you come across to your listeners.

(3) Know why you are talking. Have a clear point of view of your subject.

(4) Know what you want your listeners to do. Be ready to tell them what is in it for them.

2. *Inhibiting physical energy.* Communicators thrive on energy: No energy—No power. The goal is to be as natural in front of a group as you are talking to a friend. Use your natural gestures. Move around. Have solid eye contact. We will study more on this later.

3. *Complicating the simple.* Most presentations fail because they are too complicated. You must learn how to take the complex and make it simple to follow and remember. Develop a clear point of view. Keep it short. Make your point and get on with it. Repeat key ideas. What one, two, or three main points do you want people to remember?

4. *Assuming the presentation is like a written report.* The spoken medium is nearly the polar opposite of the written medium. Be careful of information-only presentations. Work from note concepts. These notes trigger thoughts you can talk about from thirty seconds to five minutes. Develop spontaneity. Work on mental control. We will provide more direction later for writing for the eye and ear.

5. *Lack of the right preparation.* Content alone will not carry you. Preparation provides confidence, and confidence provides enthusiasm. Prepare yourself to speak. Polish your skills before you are in the spotlight. Rehearse. Rehearse. Rehearse. You want to sound organized, not memorized. Visualize yourself in action. See yourself happy and excited.

6. *Neglecting the importance of visuals.* Seeing is more than believing. You can say "67 percent" and "33 percent," but a pie chart will have a greater impact. Think visually about your subject. Turn ideas into pictures. We will talk more later about how to choose the right visual aids, how to use the tools, use your face, arms, eyes, and hands.

7. *Neglecting today's technology.* To enhance your presentation, use technology and computer software. Use video and audio to watch and listen to yourself. Note the best and worst things you did. Get

feedback on how you came across to others. Watch how other present-ers make their subjects come alive. Note your progress. We will add specifics on this later!

Cornerstones for Your Audience

What Is Your Point of View? Once you have completed the interpre-tation of a passage of God's Word, you have reached some conclusions or come to a point of view on that particular passage. We will study more later about interpretation of Scripture. For right now, you have a feeling, opinion or attitude about the text and the subject. Now, as a "whole brain commu-nicator" your responsibility is to serve as the bridge between the text and the times. Before you begin to frame or organize your message, you must be able to answer three questions:

You must learn how to take the complex and make it simple to follow and remember. Develop a clear point of view. Keep it short. Make your point and get on with it. Repeat key ideas. What one, two, or three main points do you want people to remember?

1. How do I feel about my subject?
2. Why am I going to speak about this subject?
3. What is the state of current affairs about this subject?

If your listeners say, "So what?" then you have failed to convey your point of view. In other words, at some point in your application, you have to bring it down to the listener's level, so that he or she can see how they can live that out in their everyday lives. We will cover more on application later.

What Is My Audience's DNA? How do they feel about me?
- Demographics—Age, occupation, level of responsibility, socioeconomics
- Needs—What are their interests?
- Attitudes—How do they feel about the subject? What moti-vates them?

What Are the Action Steps When the Message Is Completed? We do not speak merely to inform but to impact and influence. There needs to be at least one general action step and one specific action step.

What Are the Benefits for the Listener? If each person listens to your message and does what you suggest, how will he or she be better off? Give the audience at least three resulting benefits for every presentation you make.

Create for Your Audience

Imagination is the "bridge" between the ancient past and the contemporary present. There is a vast difference between fantasy and imagination. Warren Wiersbe once described fantasy as "Disney World" and imagination as "Epcot Center." Disney World causes one to escape the real world while Epcot causes one to engage a brand new world.

Ministers are to preach the gospel in such a way as to help people see a new world with Christ in the center. One of the reasons the great entertainment centers of the world can charge exorbitant prices and still turn away thousands of people is creativity. The reason so many people sit sanctimoniously in our sanctuaries half asleep is because ministers often do and say the same things the same way while expecting a miracle on Sunday. Our culture demands creativity.

Preachers need to remember they do not see the world as other people see it but as they see it. We assume that the world is the way we speak it, that reality matches the metaphors we live by. Effective communicators understand how listeners imagine or view their world. The sacred responsibility of the preacher is to use biblically guided imagination to cross the bridge from the past to the present. The danger lies in the preacher's mind serving as a "filter" or "paradigm" to bring the accurate sacred message of the scriptural passage into the arena of ideas today.

Imagination is the imagining function of the mind. It is thinking by seeing, as contrasted with reasoning. Imagination puts flesh and clothes on naked ideas and facts. It makes the unknown known and the unseen seen. Warren Wiersbe declares:

> "Imagineering" a text means trying to see it in a contemporary setting and identifying in it images that speak to people today. We must take care, though, in presenting this contemporary image that we don't abandon the original image or alter it to suit our purposes because we're preaching God's Word and not our own ideas. The modern

equivalent is the point of contact for the text and never a substitute."
(Wiersbe, 286-287)

The imaginative mind sees how different facts and ideas can be
mixed together to build a sermon. Just as a contractor knows how
to pull together blueprints, brick, sand, and wood in order to build
a house, the creative preacher knows how to tie together the parts of
exegesis to form a "meaning" and the different aspects of homiletics
to form a "message." The creative preacher powerfully connects every
word of the message to the next to form sentences packed with pictures
for the modern mind to understand eternal truth. Imagination arouses
faith in God and His Word. Imagination makes history come alive
today. Imagination is one of the strongest allies of the sermonizer to
change lives forever.

In a famous US court case that was dramatized in a movie, an
inventor who created the intermittent windshield wiper defended
himself against engineers that stole his idea. They claimed he used
materials that were already in existence and therefore did not invent
their use. The inventor called for a book to be read. He stated to the
judge that although each word of the book was common, the meaning
of the words put together was the result of the author's creativity. The
inventor won his case that he had used the common building blocks
of engineering to create something new. Likewise, this is every creative
minister's challenge.

Words are outward, vocal expressions of hidden thoughts in a
person's mind. Creativity and imagination can make unseen thoughts
visible. We cannot see the thoughts of God. They are hidden from
us. But, God revealed those thoughts through the life of Jesus. Jesus
became both the outward visual and vocal expressions of the hidden
thoughts of God. As sermonizers, we strive to help people who are
blind to the truths and thoughts of God in His Word to see visions
in their minds and the difference Jesus Christ will make in their lives.

Creativity is the product of imagination. It is the end result of the
imaginative process. Wiersbe wrote:

Creativity is the result of the imagination bringing together both science
and art and allowing them to interact. Creativity is both left-brain and

right-brain, both analysis and synthesis. Analysis deals with facts and concepts, synthesis with truths and pictures. The scientist in you takes the text apart (exegesis) and the poet in you puts it back together (homiletics) so that concepts become pictures and information becomes motivation. (Wiersbe, 292)

Imagination and creativity are to be used all along the way of sermon preparation. Just as prayer keeps the proclaimer related rightly to God, imagination and creativity will keep the proclaimer relevant to the world. To be effective gospel communicators, preachers stay in touch with the eternal world above them—God, the temporary world around them—nature and humanity, the pragmatic world within them—the body, mind, and spirit, and the life-changing world of the Bible. The imaginative evangelist or pastor has the distinct ability to pull all of these worlds together into an effective preaching ministry.

Words are outward, vocal expressions of hidden thoughts in a person's mind. Creativity and imagination can make unseen thoughts visible.

Do you ever get tired of going through the same regimen, routine, and ritual? You know what this routine is. You wake up. Take a shower. Go to work. Have some lunch. Work some more. Go home. Eat dinner. Watch some television. Read a book. Go to bed. The next day you wake up. Take a shower. Go to work. Have some lunch. Work some more. Go home. Eat dinner. Watch some television. Read a book. Go to bed. Do the same again and again.

The net effect of this monotony is that pastors, staff members, and ministers can feel like they are sleepwalking through life, looking for adventure and excitement. Conventional wisdom says the problem is relational. If you were married to that *other* person with those looks or that bank account, then you would have a spring in your step. Conventional wisdom says the problem is occupational. If you worked for that church or served in *that* community with *that* kind of influence, then you would have it all.

If your life luster has dimmed, you could be neglecting one of the greatest qualities of human existence, the God-given quality made available to each of us when we were created in the very image of Creator God. This is what I call the "missing link." Bureaucracy kills it. Systems stifle it. Education squelches it. The Church is silent about it. What is the missing link? Creativity!

Just the mention of the term "creativity" bombards our brains with excuses. We say something like, "I am not creative." We say creativity is for dancers, songwriters, authors, musicians, and artists. As we walk through life and work for God, we develop a "creative cramp." We trade dreaming for dogma, move from laughter to logic and from using our imaginations to memorization. Ministers often live their lives on "pause." They copy something rather than create something. This breaks the heart of God. Let's hit the "play" button and get off "pause"! God wants all of us to ride on the crest of creativity. Let's take off our floaties and stop splashing around in the shallow waters of sameness.

Three one-word questions regarding creativity:

Why? We should be creative because God invented creativity. He thought it up. It was His idea. The fifth word in the Bible is "created." "In the beginning God created . . ." Everything God touches is innovative. How can we claim to be connected with Someone like God and be so boring in our ministries and so predictable? Why do so many ministers live in prison cells called "ruts"? Why do we not live the life of creative innovation and spontaneity?

In Ephesians 5:1 we read, "Be imitators of God." The term "imitator" means to mimic. When I am being creative, I am mimicking God. Jesus modeled creativity in His ministry. "He did not speak to them without a parable" an illustration (Mt 13:34). He never used the same approach twice. He drew in the sand. Picked up a coin. Pointed to a sower. Painted pictures. Taught from boats and beaches to hillsides and private gatherings. Turned over tables.

People need creativity. Because we are made in the image of our Creator we yearn and burn to be communicated with in a creative way. God used a piece of fruit for Adam. A slingshot for David. A whale for Jonah. Salt for Lot. An altar for Abraham. A cross for the world.

I am not advocating a particular kind of model for church growth and evangelism. I simply believe *we have been empowered by God to be creative geniuses.*

We must use our creativity in our context. It does not matter what style of church we have as long as we are biblical in our approach to creatively communicate God's Word to unique people. I am not advocating that you bounce off the walls in your worship. Your creativity may best be expressed by the rearrangement of the platform. Or, speaking earlier rather than later. Or, having the choir go to the audience after they sing. Or, video in the middle of the sermon. You will have to find what it is that keeps you from being caught in the cell of predictability.

It is easy to get caught in a system when you have success. You begin to think the system is the answer when it was your creativity that brought you to the place where you are. Get creative! Stay creative!

Where? Ed Young, Jr., speaking at the Southern Baptist Pastors Conference in 2002, stated something I would paraphrase as, "We need creativity on the marital front. Most couples get off the cruise of their honeymoon. Most wives think they are going to cruise deeper into a creative realm of romance, but the husband has dropped anchor in Boredom Bay. He is a pastor, teacher, or evangelist now. He is building his church or ministry. He gets up, takes a shower, goes to work, has lunch, works some more, has dinner, watches television, reads, and goes to bed."

We need creativity on the church front. The Church should be the most innovative organization in the universe. The most creative ideas should come from Christians. Christians should be cranking out the tapes and books on creativity.

Some time ago, my wife and I went to Las Vegas while we were ministering in a nearby state. No, we did not go to gamble! But, while we were there, I noticed the signage in the city. There are all kinds of signs and all colors of signs. It dawned on me that Las Vegas does not have much to say, but they sure do know how to say it. The local church, however, has the most important truths to say, but we do not know how to say it. We need to learn how to say it, to communicate the gospel.

"Where the Spirit of the Lord is, there is liberty" (2 Co 3:17). There is constant change going on. Church should be a great place to go in the community. People should be standing in line, come with anticipation, talk about it to their friends before the service begins. If we are mirroring our Creator, then this kind of scenario will take place.

How? We are to listen to God's cheer. Did you realize God is cheering for you? God is saying, "You've got it, now use it." I challenge you to pray a high-octane prayer. Ask God to make you more creative. Connect with creative people. Who is helping you? Who is mentoring you? Who is pouring into your life? Who are your role models?

We need to go through labor and delivery. It is time to become pregnant with ideas and give birth to them. Work and creativity are inseparable. Creativity is like conception, labor, and delivery. In fact, creativity is like giving to birth to barbwire. Most have us have creative ideas, but most of us are not willing to pay the price to birth them. We would rather follow a stale model of ministry than to develop a patent on our own ministry.

Creative people make it look easy. The easier something looks in ministry, the more hard work that was done behind the scenes. We have to stay at it to birth it. What would have happened if God had stopped His idea of Christ coming to earth to die for our sins? We would have been lost for eternity. We must build in "creativity time"— blocks of time to pray, think, conceptualize, brainstorm, and write before we make it happen. Pastors can do creativity as a team and not just by themselves.

We should install a "confusion principle" in our lives. Our bodies are a great example. When I go to the health club on a regular basis, I purposely change up my workout. If you stay with the same workout too long, or workout the same muscle group each day, your muscles will not develop properly.

It is important to change up parts of our lives. This is one reason why successful evangelists make excellent pastors. Over the years, they have mastered the confusion principle. They have learned to be effective even though they have different surroundings, circumstances, and audiences every week of their lives.

Confuse your church from time to time! Change the bulletin. Change the worship. Change the service. Change the staff schedule. Creativity produces growth in worship, evangelism, vision, our gifts, and leadership. And, creativity makes God smile.

Creativity is the secret between winning and losing, between growing and shrinking, between sleepwalking and living. Behind every winner is the burning desire of optimism and enthusiasm toward the rewards of success and the penalties of failure, toward the solution and not the problem, and toward the answer in place of the question. In the audio series entitled "Psychology of Winning," Dennis Waitley has said:

Losers	Winners
See thunderstorms	See rainbows
See icy streets	Put on their ice skates
Complain	Train and gain
Take chances	Make choices
Are aggressive	Are assertive
Seek attention	Earn respect
Fix the blame	Fix what caused the problem
Live in the past	Learn from the past, working in the present toward the future
Make promises they often break	Make commitments they keep
React negatively	Respond effectively

Losing and winning is a habit in life. Each of us needs to develop our own software-thinking package and download it into the mainframe of our lives. From time to time, we need to upgrade our thinking processes in order to stay in touch with our rapidly-changing world.

Leaders whom people respect and follow are those who are able to communicate effectively. They have a dynamic presence. If we desire to make a difference, we have to learn to communicate with a powerful presence. We must be able to communicate what we want to get done in the church, in ministry and in life.

Visualization: Another form of imagination is visualization. Maxwell Maltz, author of *Psycho-Cybernetics*, captured a truth that can transform how we process and prepare for events in our lives. He discovered that the mind cannot tell the difference between an actual experience and one that is vividly imagined. The inner brain—our emotional part and the gatekeeper for the analytical outer brain—

cannot tell the difference between fantasy and reality. That is why a scary movie can frighten us even though we know it is not reality. In the same way, the more we imagine giving a particular presentation, the less fearful it becomes for us because the mind believes it has already said and done it. We can turn an upcoming fearful event into something pleasant. In order for the imagination to become vivid, it must be filled with emotion. By visualizing it, we can make ourselves feel the success of an upcoming presentation. (Decker, 212, 222)

Cluster for Your Audience

Those who are the most creative have a structure to their presentation. Those who do not have a structure are slaves to chaos. We must be focused on our destination. How many times have we listened to a message and said at the end, "What was the main point?" "What did he really say?" When this happens, the speaker failed to create a powerful message.

Every message must be packaged in some creative way in order for the audience to grasp its meaning and be motivated by it. The biblical text determines the substance of the sermon. The sermonizer determines the structure of the sermon. Rick Warren states, "The crowd does not determine whether or not you speak the truth: The truth is not optional. But your audience does determine which truths you choose to speak about." (Warren, 228)

There are at least eight thought-provoking questions for a presenter to ask during the packaging of effective messages, some of which are:

1. **To whom will I be speaking?** (1 Co 9:22-23)
2. **What does the passage say about their needs?** (Lk 4:18-19; 2 Tim 3:16)
3. **What is the most practical way to say it?** (Jas 1:22; Tit 2:1) Give specific actions. Show them how to do it. Think zip code.
4. **What is the most positive way to say it?** (Pro 16:21; Col 4:5-6)
5. **What is the most encouraging way to say it?** (Pro 12:25; Rom 15:4)
6. **What is the simplest way to say it?** (1 Co 2:1, 4) Simple does not mean shallow. Avoid using religious terms. Keep the outline

simple. Write the sermon into a single sentence. Prepare the sermon outline in the present tense.

7. **What is the most personal way to say it?** (2 Co 6:11; 1 Th 2:8)
8. **What is the most interesting way to say it?** (Col 4:5-6)

In order for the contemporary communicator to be relevant in a secular society, there are three all-encompassing questions to answer before presenting the gospel:

1. **What is the point of the passage?** This is accomplished through investigation and interpretation by the presenter.
2. **What are the pictures for the people?** Creativity and imagination build the bridge from the ancient text to the present day.
3. **What is the package for the presenter?** The presenter will have to decide, based on his or her audience, exactly how the message is to be structured for maximum results.

The following comparison illustrates the differences between the preparation and the packaging of the message.

PREPARATION OF SERMON	PACKAGING OF SERMON
FACTS	TRUTHS
PAST EVENTS	PRESENT EXPERIENCES
DATED HISTORY	TIMELESS TRUTHS
THE TEXT	THE TIMES
INTERPRETATION	APPLICATION
ORDER OF THE PASSAGE	NOT NECESSARILY ORDER OF THE PASSAGE
INCLUDES ALL MATERIAL	SELECTIVE
NOT UNIFIED	UNIFIED

Compose For Your Audience

We compose the message with the desire to involve the people. While writing the message, imagine it being spoken to the audience. Does it sound good? Will it involve the audience?

If our desire is to reach listeners, spend a great deal of time listening. We must know our listeners and their needs, wants, and perspectives. To have a powerful presence, we need to become excellent listeners.

Do you know the options for involving people? Do you know the three different forms of questions? Do you know how to wake people up in your audience without them knowing what you are doing? Do you know the two times in your presentation your audience is most attentive and what to do at the other times?

The goal is to involve as many people as possible every time you speak to them. We need to engage the whole person when we speak, or we will miss the opportunity to persuade them and motivate them at the conclusion of the message. The more involved the listeners are, the more likely we are to convince them of our message. There are eight basic involvement techniques:

1. **Drama.** Telling a moving story dramatically. Create a strong opening by announcing a serious problem, ask a rhetorical question dramatically, make a startling statement dramatically. Use intense emotion, add color or smell through words, end the presentation with a dramatic quote or story.

2. **Eye communication.** Survey your entire audience at the beginning of your presentation. Keep your listeners engaged by maintaining three- to six-second contact with as many as possible.

3. **Movement.** Change the dynamics of your presentation by purposeful movement. Never back away from your listeners. Move toward them at the beginning and the end of your presentation. When someone is sleeping, just move to an area of the room where you have not been before or move toward the person sleeping. If the person sleeping looks up at you, be looking directly at him or her.

4. **Visuals.** Use different visuals. Practice in advance so transitions will be smooth. We will cover transitions thoroughly later in one entire "law."

5. **Ask questions.** There are several different kinds of questions:
   - Rhetorical questions—Ask a question but do not expect an answer.
   - Ask for a show of hands on different issues.
   - Ask for a volunteer—Adrenaline will flow through the audience.

6. **Demonstrations.** Plan ahead, gauging the time but using it wisely. Get a volunteer from the audience.

7. **Think of your audience interest level.** Concentrate on listener techniques during the middle of your presentation. The interest of the audience is always the highest at the beginning and end of the presentation, so maintain a high level of personal interest in the middle of the session.

8. **Use humor.** Make it appropriate and relevant to your point of view. If you make a bad mistake, laugh at yourself. Be tasteful but human (Decker, 139-143). One later "law" is devoted to humor.

As we strive to communicate to the Googlers, Gutenbergers or both, let's remember that we are privileged to hold in our hands the Word of God and have a holy responsibility to proclaim its content with the highest form of integrity. Even though we face a more challenging audience today, we can still be successful in our communication worldwide, to young and old alike.

Left Brain
(Principles/Rational)

Right Brain
(Pictures/Relational)

LAW

5

PEOPLE NEED EARS
TURNED INTO EYES FOR
THE PRESENTATION

If I speak with the tongues of men and of angels,
but do not have love, I have become a noisy gong
or a clanging cymbal. (1 Co 13:1)

At a convention of professionals where I was invited by the organizers, I seated myself next to the renowned evangelist Reinhard Bonnke, who was scheduled to give a "motivational" speech laced with Christian themes to bring the Gospel into this secular setting. Our assistants sat in suits alongside us, all of us focused to convey in appearance, word and deed our respect for those attending, in order to make the widest opening possible for this secular audience to receive the Gospel message.

The first speaker of the evening was a renowned doctor. A great introduction was made by an emcee who understood the reason for an introduction—to give the audience a reason to listen to the speaker. However, the speaker did not meet expectations. He restarted his presentation more than once; showed meaningless, cluttered power point slides; read parts of his speech in a monotone; interspersed the rest of it with filler words and stammers that prolonged him past his end time;

and made feeble jokes before he finally, mercifully stepped down. He bombed while speaking to his own crowd.

Up to the stage stepped the great Bonnke, to speak to an audience completely foreign to him. He revitalized the audience, verbalized the Gospel with tremendous visual word pictures, then gave an altar call. As I recall, roughly one hundred people came to Christ that evening. The communicator who was not on his home turf is the one who hit the homerun!

In any setting, the difference between a leader who people respect and follow is the ability to communicate effectively. Such leaders have a dynamic presence. The effectiveness of your communications determines the effectiveness of your life. If you desire to make a difference, learn to communicate with a powerful presence.

The power of the presentation is derived by the person who gives it. If the preacher is boring to the congregation, people will think God is boring. Some ministers have style without substance while others have substance without style. Preachers need to be able to combine substance with style in their preaching. The Christian and non-Christian alike are searching for truth in a generation preoccupied with self, avarice, and greed.

Substance is "what" is said, and style is "how" it is said. There is a certain amount of style in the packaging of a sermon. In John 12:49, Jesus said, "For I did not speak on My own initiative, but the Father Himself who sent Me has given Me a commandment as to what to say and what to speak." In other words, Jesus was led by the Father in all aspects of His speaking.

What do we mean by the delivery of a message? It simply means to deliver "into the possession of the person for whom it was intended." Delivery refers to the methods by which you communicate "what" you have to say to the "who." It is possible for the preacher to speak the message, use up a portion of time, give an invitation, and still not accomplish the intended purpose of the sermon. Every time we stand before an audience, we will use vocal, verbal, and visual techniques to capture the attention of the audience and to bring them along to the conclusion of the presentation. We do not need to know every scientific fact about sight and sound. We do need to know how to leverage them to make them work *for* us and not *against* us.

The message is verbalized, vocalized, visualized, and vitalized. Many ministers of the gospel spend most of their time thinking about what they are going to say to the audience, yet studies have concluded that the decision-making process of people is determined first by visual, second by vocal and third by verbal cues. Visual cues account for 55 percent of the audience's decision, sounds and tones account for 38 percent, and the actual words of the presentation account for only 7 percent. This data further illustrates that the average person is persuaded more by feelings than by facts. The visual cues the speaker gives to the audience are positively or negatively persuasive. Mannerisms, gestures, head movements, facial expressions, platform movement, eye contact, and clothing project the overall presence of the presenter (Arredondo, 65).

The vocal effectiveness of the presenter is determined by quality, intonation, pauses, and fillers. The voice should project the different "landscapes" of the sermon with changes in volume, speed and tone according to the content of the message. Pauses help the preacher and the audience to catch up with the message. Fillers are avoided as they are distracting to the listeners.

The verbal persuasion of the presenter is greatly determined by the choice of words and phrases. Emotive words drive the theme of the message home. Greater still is the communicator's enthusiasm about the message. Every word and phrase of the minister should be chosen for maximum impact because we are not called to impress people but to influence their decision-making for Christ. If an evangelist or a pastor says one thing but the voice communicates another, confusion results in the minds of the audience. (Arredondo, 77-79)

Just as there are unique styles of clothing to cover our physical bodies, there are also unique styles of communication to clothe our thoughts. Here are some general rules:

1. Never read from or memorize a manuscript
2. Never speak in an angry tone
3. Never point at people
4. Never embarrass people
5. Respect people and their time

6. View yourself as a role model

7. Say "thank you" for having the opportunity of speaking to them

8. Start on time and finish on time

The unseen spiritual world is more resourceful than the seen world of exegetical exactitude in the evangelist's or pastor's office. The same Holy Spirit who moved on the apostles and prophets of old will illuminate our minds today. John MacArthur writes:

> No clear understanding of Scripture leading to powerful preaching is possible without the Spirit's work of illumination. Powerful preaching occurs only when a Spirit-illumined man of God expounds clearly and compelling God's Spirit-inspired revelation in Scripture to a Spirit-illumined congregation. (MacArthur, 102-103)

When we preach the Gospel, the message is not only verbalized, vocalized and visualized, but it is vitalized. We don't have to *revitalize* a church that stays *vitalized* in the power of the Holy Spirit. We often underestimate the role and goals of the Holy Spirit and overestimate our skills and gifts in ministry. I have heard presentations that were exegetically sound but dead. The Holy Spirit turns a manuscript into a message and a sermon into a sword.

There is a difference between inspiration and illumination. Inspiration is the process by which men "inscripturated" the revelation of God. The Apostle Paul needed inspiration to write the revelation of God—things previously unknown. *Inspiration* was the vehicle to reveal eternal truth from God to us in the Bible. *Illumination* is the vehicle to fully ascertain the correct interpretation and application of a particular pericope, or Scripture selection. The anointing or illumination of the Holy Spirit will teach the meaning of the Word of God during the minister's study (1 Jn. 2:20, 27). The Word of God comes alive for the minister when illumination becomes a part of the preparation for effective evangelistic sermons.

It is imperative that the preacher not underestimate the role of the Holy Spirit during the preparation and the proclamation of the message. The main sin in the Old Testament was the rejection of God the Father while the main sin in the New Testament was the rejection of Christ the Son. Is it possible that the main sin of the contemporary Church is the rejection of the Third Person, the Holy Spirit?

In the ministry in general and preaching in particular, the pendulum usually sways from one extreme to the other. On one side is "escapism," and the other is "extremism." (Olford, 30). In other words, preachers tend to ignore the role of the Holy Spirit in ministry or tend to go overboard to the point of manipulating people. The Holy Spirit is a gift, not a toy! There needs to be biblical balance in the private arena of preparation and the public arena of proclamation.

Only the Holy Spirit can transform a manuscript into a message. Only the Holy Spirit can bring together our text, topic, theme, thoughts, and thrust to eternally change lives. There is a difference between the "filling" of the Spirit and the "anointing" of the Spirit. For example, Jesus was filled with the Spirit from conception, but He was anointed by the Spirit before He began His public ministry (Lk. 1:35, 2:52; Acts 10:38). The difference is between having the Holy Spirit as a resident and having the Holy Spirit as president.

In 1998, I was privileged to conduct a nationwide conference call with Bible college and seminary presidents with the late Dr. Bill Bright. During that call, Dr. Bright challenged the college presidents to schedule in their preaching programs a time when students who were to be preachers would be challenged to fast and pray forty days before graduating to preach. Dr. Bright quoted that following the forty days of Christ's temptation, He came to the synagogue and announced: "The Spirit of the Lord is upon me, because he has anointed me to preach the gospel" (Lk. 4:18; Isa 61:1-2).

In that moment, I realized that Jesus chose what words He would say on the first time He ever stood in a Jewish synagogue to preach. He made his opening statement emphatic so no one could doubt the divine calling or the divine task. The anointing of the Holy Spirit enables us to preach God's Word with God's breath upon it.

On another occasion, I heard Dr. Jack Hayford state that there are people who preach God's Word with their breath, and there are preachers who preach God's Word with His breath. It is His breath that is the anointing in preaching the Gospel.

What does the Holy Spirit or the anointing of the Holy Spirit have to do with "turning eyes into ears"? The Holy Spirit turns a manuscript into a message and information into inspiration. When we study the Word of God, the Holy Spirit: (1) Illuminates the passages for our presentations; (2) Infuses power into our presentations; (3) Impacts the people through our presentations.

THE PREREQUISITES TO THE ANOINTING
(LK 3:21-22)

Scripture states: "Now it came about when all the people were baptized, that Jesus also was baptized, and while He was praying, heaven was opened, and the Holy Spirit descended upon Him in bodily form like a dove, and a voice came out of heaven, 'This is My beloved Son, in whom I am well-pleased" (Mt 3:17). For the preacher to be anointed by the Holy Spirit, there must be:

Sanctification: "I am well-pleased." We are to be more concerned about what the Heavenly Father says about us than anyone else. The one who pleases others still may not have pleased God, but the one who pleases God doesn't have to worry about pleasing others.

Submission: "Jesus was baptized." Jesus did not place Himself above the common people. There is no place for arrogance in the ministry or the messenger.

Supplication: "He was praying." Prayer is what keeps the heavens open. When the preacher closes his or her heart in prayer, the heavens eventually close as well.

THE PICTURE OF THE ANOINTING

During the baptism of Jesus Christ, the Holy Spirit descended in bodily form like a dove upon Him. The "Dove" is a symbol of:

Peace (Ge 8:11): Noah, the dove, and olive branch

Purity (Mt 10:16): Jesus instructed His disciples to be as harmless as doves.

Passion (Eze 7:16): The cooing of the dove is used in the Scripture to signify suffering, mourning and passion.

Power (Ac 1:8; Lk 24:49): The outpouring of the Holy Spirit was accompanied with power (Olford, 220-22).

THE PURPOSE OF THE ANOINTING

Jesus said the anointing of the Spirit is for the message, to preach the gospel (Lk. 3:18, 22); and for the ministry, to the poor…to the captives…to the blind…and to those who are downtrodden (Lk. 3:18). God desires for your message and ministry to be anointed by the Holy Spirit. The preaching of the gospel has results. Some are glad and others are mad at what they heard in the sermon. At the conclusion of Jesus' first sermon, some marveled at the message and others were mad at the Messenger. In fact, Jesus' life was threatened as a result of the sermon. The anointing of the Holy Spirit makes the difference in every sermon and in every worship service.

THE PRIORITIES OF THE ANOINTING
(EPH 5:16-22; 6:5, 12)

Imagine a man who has his first, brand new automobile. He takes the car to his friends. He shows off the color, the interior, the radio— all of the car. However, the man does not realize there is an engine in the car, so everywhere he goes, he pushes the car. He enjoys going down the hill, but he knows he has to push it back up. The blessing of the car has become a burden to him.

You may think no one would be that stupid. Yet, a lot of Christians try to push themselves in their service rather than being empowered by the Holy Spirit. They are just like the man trying to push the car everywhere he goes. Christianity is not a burden but a blessing. Your Christian life is not monotonous but momentous.

REASONS FOR THE SPIRIT-FILLED LIFE (EPH 5:16)
Obedience

"Be filled with the Holy Spirit" (Eph 5:18). If we are not filled with the Holy Spirit, we are disobeying God. This verse is written in the imperative. This is more than a blessing to enjoy, it is a command to obey. This verse is in the present tense. God is not interested in whether we *were* filled with the Holy Spirit. He wants to know are we are *now* filled with the Holy Spirit. This verse literally says "being you, being filled." It is plural in number, not singular. It is passive in voice. This means it is not something we do but something we attain. God wants to fill us with the Holy Spirit. We do not have to persuade God to fill us; we need to permit God to fill us.

Obligations (Eph 5:19, 22, 25; 6:5, 12, 19)

1. *Worship Life* (5:19). The worst that could be said of a song would not be due to a wrong key but due to singing it to the wrong person. Our singing is to be to the Lord. There is nothing worse than a church full of half-empty people trying their hardest to "overflow."

2. *Wedded Life* (5:22, 25). In this age of militant feminism, how is the wife going to submit to her husband? By being filled with the Holy Spirit. This is not addressing "inferiority" of women. A woman is superior to a man in being a woman, and a man is superior to a woman in being a man. God made the man and woman different in order to make them one, yet God put headship in the home. Anything with two heads is a freak, and anything with no head is dead. The Word of God is stricter for the husband. In verse 25, the husband is to love his wife as Christ loved the Church. Jesus loved the Church sacrificially, steadfastly, and satisfyingly and so is the man to do unto his wife. The man can only do this through the power of the Holy Spirit.

3. *Work Life* (6:5). When we go to work, we are to work for a boss as if the boss were Jesus Christ. Some may say, "That creep!" But, if the people who hear the Word of God on Sunday lived it on Monday, then the people in the workplace, creeps and all, would believe what we preach on Sunday. We live in a day when everyone wants their rights. If we teach a generation to be selfish regarding their rights, then we will have a revolution. If we teach people to be diligent about their responsibilities, then we will have a revival.

4. *War Life* (6:12). We are in a battle for the souls of men and women. Satan laughs at our plans and sneers at our intentions.

5. *Witness Life* (6:19). Let us rather die than be sentenced to preach the gospel without the anointing and infilling of the Holy Spirit. Let us teach others to rather die than try to be a Christian without the Holy Spirit.

Opportunity (Eph 5:16)

We need to redeem the time. Any day that is not a Spirit-filled day is a day lost forever. When I stand before Christ, I will give account for this day. Unless my day was a Spirit-filled day, then it is wood, hay, and stubble. We live in a later age than we may think. This life is too short, eternity too long, lives too precious, and the gospel too wonderful for us to be living carnal, without the constant presence of the Holy Spirit.

The Requirements for the Spirit-Filled Life (Eph 5:18)
Complete Surrender

"Be filled *with* the Spirit," does not mean "be filled by the Spirit." It is not that the Holy Spirit is putting wisdom, power, and discernment *into* you. Your body is a temple. The Holy Spirit wants to *dwell in* your mortal body.

Continual Surrender

There must be a continual yielding to the Spirit. Why did Paul say, "Do not drink with wine in excess, but be filled with the Spirit"? Why did he not say, "Do not steal, but be filled with the Spirit"?

Our text is speaking in contrast. The devil's intoxication is a substitute for the Holy Spirit's intoxication. It is a greater sin not to "be filled with the Holy Spirit" than it would be to get drunk. The sins of omission are greater than the sins of commission. I am not being soft on alcohol. No Spirit-filled person would want to be drunk anyway.

Paul is also talking in comparison. A person gets drunk by drinking. How does a person stay drunk? He keeps on drinking. How do people "be filled with the Holy Spirit"? They drink. How do people continue to be filled? They keep on drinking or being filled with the Holy Spirit. The problem today is that many have sobered up!

Conscious Surrender—Anointing

The anointing is the special touch for the specific task. Every time before preaching, we humbly request the Lord to freshly anoint us with special touch for a specific task. It is the power of the Holy Spirit that illuminates the mind, heart and soul to the eternal gospel. As we prepare and preach, we execute with excellence the verbalized, vocalized and visualized elements of our messages. At the same time, we offer our sermon as a sacrifice to be consumed by Holy Spirit fire. Our role is to fulfill God's goal and our part is to help fulfill what is in God's heart.

I will never forget as long as I live walking around the perimeter of more than 600,000 people at a Reinhard Bonnke crusade in Abuja, Nigeria. While Evangelist Bonnke preached the Gospel with great clarity and conviction, I walked with one of his long-term team members all the way around the outskirts of this massive crowd that had gathered in an open field. The sun had already set, and the stars shined bright in the Milky Way around us.

When I finally got to the very back of this enormous crowd, the stage and its lighting looked very small to the naked eye. Yet, I could hear Reinhard preaching with magnificent clarity due to the state-of-the-art sound system his supporters had provided for these meetings. I remember looking at a mother holding her precious baby, staring toward the stage, unable to see the speaker from that distance, and listening to every word of Bonnke's message. As I watched her intense attention to the "preached Word," I was reminded that it is the communicator's responsibility to make sure that the audience hears, understands and responds to the message. We are called to turn ears into the eyes so our audience can go from hearing the Word to believing the Word.

Left Brain
(Principles/Rational)

Right Brain
(Pictures/Relational)

Law 1:	Fill the Pulpit	Law 2:	Buy on Emotion
Law 3:	Begin with the End in Mind	Law 4:	Giving Birth to Barbwire
Law 5:	Turn Ears to Eyes	**Law 6:**	**Pray Yourself to Life**
Law 7:	The Great Sword of Truth	Law 8:	Mind Craves Order
Law 9:	The Private Discipline	Law 10:	The Picture Gallery
Law 11:	The Clock and the Crowd	Law 12:	Knowing the Audience
Law 13:	Offensively Equals Defensively	Law 14:	Timing Is Everything
Law 15:	From Reasons to Visions	Law 16:	Becoming Unpredictable
Law 17:	Polished Transitions	Law 18:	Humor to Heart
Law 19:	The First Ninety Seconds	Law 20:	Give More than Expected

LAW

6

STUDY YOURSELF TO DEATH,
PRAY YOURSELF BACK TO LIFE

*Be diligent to present yourself approved to God as a workman
who does not need to be ashamed, accurately handling
the word of truth. (2 Tim 2:14-15)*

ears ago at a denominational missions conference, pastors together with the missionaries they had visited took turns giving their best presentations about their part of the world. The program droned on with report after report, until the packed house of pastors and leaders began to shift in their chairs. The audience had a program and knew that the evening would be capped off by an eighty-year-old missionary to China. Although everyone in the room respected him, no one was looking forward to another report.

Finally, the emcee called the elder minister to the podium with a brief explanation of how this man was kicked out of China, the place of his calling, when the communists took over. The man shuffled to the front and looked at the crowd of bored and restless leaders. His eyes brimmed with tears, and he threw back his head to give a one-word message. He raised his hands toward heaven and from a broken heart cried a one-word sermon with a shout: "CHINA!" The ministers in the audience, jarred from their boredom and apathy, fell to their knees and began to pray and cry out to God as this great, aged preacher made his way back to his chair.

No matter how great we are, how big our church, how renowned our ministry, we cannot afford to address any audience or make any message preparation without a "spirit of prayer" in our hearts. It is prayer that gives us the wisdom of our words, prayer that moves the hearts of our audience, prayer that allows us to make crucial adjustments in our presentation that rules, or ruins, the hour.

"A preacher who is not praying in the ministry is playing in the ministry." (Ravenhill, 47) The minister "does not stop to pray: he simply does not stop from prayer." (Quayle, 261). The preacher studies to learn how to pray. Jesus did not teach His disciples how to preach but how to pray. The emphasis is sometimes more on how to preach rather than how to pray in order to preach. Prayer is a critical element in effective communication of the Gospel.

Our presentations are not simply about the temporal but the eternal. On the surface, the secularist would not recognize this "prayer law" as necessary to building the bridge between the Gutenberg and Google worlds. Nevertheless, prayer is not replaced by expanding technology or breakthroughs in molecular biology nor does it recognize geographical boundaries. Every presenter of the Gospel can testify that there is a miraculous dimension that must be acknowledged even though never fully understood. This does not mean that we no longer study; neither does it mean that we no longer pray. If we are going to penetrate a secular mindset or a callous soul, then our presentations must be backed up and inundated with the power of prayer.

Pray! Pray for more workers, empowerment, boldness, miracles, open doors, the right message, clear communication, expansion of the gospel, deliverance, local church involvement, finances and salvation of the lost. Pray over and through all the steps of preparation for effective evangelistic preaching. Pray for the lost who will hear your sermon. Ask the Lord to direct every thought during your sermon preparation for the purposes of connecting, communicating and converting the lost to Christ.

The priority of the minister's prayer life will determine the power of his or her evangelism. When we study the biographies of evangelists

God used in the past, the common denominator of prominence was their priority on prayer. Mighty men and women of God will have a consistent quiet time with God.

The first area of the pastor's ministry to be developed is not the "public life" before crowds but the private life before God. This is not an exhortation for public prayer, but for the private prayer that precedes it. We are not talking about prayer for the sick, although the minister should believe God to perform such miracles. We are talking about a minister's private prayer closet.

The Reasons for an Effective Prayer Life

The first reason for developing a disciplined prayer life is for *spiritual conditioning*. The spiritual muscles of the minister grow as he or she "stretches" and "works" them out through supplication before God. The quality of the minister's quiet time will result either in spiritual strength or spiritual weakness. It is hypocritical to preach to people that we did not first pray *for*.

Second, the prayer life is for *spiritual cleansing*. Ministry travels are made up of dirty, muddy roads. Each day the soul of the minister is soiled by the world. Non-Christian attitudes can creep into the heart. Sin can be committed even in ministry. The prayer life is the time for spiritually washing the heart, mind, emotions, and will before God.

The more time spent each day in prayer, the more adjustments will be made in attitudes and actions in ministry. The heart becomes pliable. The spirit becomes teachable. The will becomes responsive.

How big is your Bible? The first part of your prayer time is to read and study the Scriptures. Every minister needs to develop a system to read and study God's Word in-depth each year.

Third, the prayer life is for *spiritual conflict*. The minister is in a spiritual war for the souls of men and women. The itinerant minister faces demonic forces every day. When preachers neglect quiet time, they are weakening their guard before Satan and his kingdom. Ministers must resolve to protect their quiet time with God regardless of the daily pressures of life and ministry. Today's minister faces the "tyranny of time." The most difficult thing to do is to prioritize prayer time every day.

The Rules for an Effective Prayer Life

There is no way to overestimate the importance of prayer (Jas 5:16-18). When we depend upon organization, we get what organization can do and that is something. When we depend upon education, we get what education can do, and that is something. When we depend upon money, we get what money can do, and that is something. When we depend upon what singing and preaching can do, we get what singing and preaching can do, and that is something. When we depend upon prayer, we get what God can do, and that is everything. Ministers need what only God can do in their lives and ministries.

The Confession Ministers Must Make (Jas 5:16)

Confession leads to consecration. Every great revival has been characterized by confession of sin before God and to one another. The healing in James 5:16 specifically deals with the restoration of the soul and spirit of a Christian. A sinful division in the Church often leads to divisiveness in the Church. Moreover, this kind of healing brings reconciliation to unhappy Christians.

Revival also comes when confession replaces criticism. There is constant temptation in the ministry to criticize fellow ministers. With humility, we are careful to listen and understand before commenting about various issues and individuals in the Church. The circle of confession follows the circle of sin. A *private sin* requires a private confession before God. A *personal sin* toward another person requires confession between you and that person. A *public sin* requires public confession. If a minister in particular or a layperson in general has sinned against the Church, then public confession is made.

The Command Ministers Should Mind (Jas 5:16)

James commands us to "pray one for another." Preachers should pray for each other. Think of other ministers and pray for them. It is hard for someone to complain about another when he or she is praying for them. When was the last time you interceded before God on behalf of another preacher? Ministers are not to be jealous of one another but are to pray daily for each other.

The Conditions Ministers Should Meet (Jas 5:16c)

"The effective prayer of a righteous man can accomplish much." Intensity is the context for this verse. The Greek term for "effective" (νεργουμένη) means "stretched-out prayer." The implication is not in length but in intensity. This is comparable to the athlete stretching for the finish line. Prayer will make you sweat. Prayer is hard work. Lukewarm prayer will not produce effective evangelism.

Ministers are to pray without ceasing (Lk 18:1; Mt 7:7-11; 1 Th 5:15). In Luke 18:1, Jesus told His disciples "not to lose heart." The same Greek term for "effective" in James 5:16 is used for "lose heart." Moreover, Jesus constantly reminded His disciples never to cease praying. Those who search for God with all of their heart will find Him (Jer 29:13).

The classic illustration of "effective" praying is Jesus' interceding in the Garden of Gethsemane. "And being in agony He was praying very fervently; and His sweat became like drops of blood, falling down upon the ground" (Lk 22:44). The Greek term for "very fervently" is the same word used in James 5:16 ("effective") and Luke 18:1 ("lose heart"). Jesus was in agony, and His soul was "stretched out" to the point that His sweat became like drops of blood. It is harder to pray to God than it is to preach His gospel. It is harder to intercede before God than it is to inspire others to serve God. If ministers are going to have the mighty anointing of the Holy Spirit upon their message and ministry, they will have to agonize in prayer before God. Leonard Ravenhill summed it up:

> No man is greater than his prayer life. The pastor who is not praying is playing; the people who are not praying are straying. We have many organizers, but few agonizers; many players and payers, few pray-ers; many singers, few clingers; lots of pastors; few wrestlers; many fears, few tears; much fashion, little passion; many interferers, few intercessors; many writers, but few fighters. Failing here, we fail everywhere. (Ravenhill, 23)

The devil is not disturbed by special singing, dynamic sermons, and services that have not been bathed in prayer for the salvation of lost people. The devil laughs over such "evangelism" efforts. The flesh does not want to pray. Prayer is spiritual warfare. Prayer is the "fight of faith." Intercession is more than merely mentioning memorized phrases.

Preachers must pray when they feel like it, when they do not feel like it, and until they do feel like it.

It is not the arithmetic of prayer or the number of times of prayer. It is not the geometry of prayer or how long the prayer is before God. It is not the rhetoric of prayer or the words used to impress God or others. It is not the music of prayer or how sweet the sound of one's voice is to the ears of God. It is not the logic of prayer or the kind of argumentation used to try to persuade God. It is the *passion* of prayer. Instead of being "through praying," ministers need to "pray through" and touch the heart of a loving God.

The Character Ministers Should Manifest (Jas 5:16d-17)

The Apostle James gives an illustration of powerful prayer through the life of Elijah. He moves from intensity to *integrity*. Elijah was a righteous man. Holy integrity before God produces power in the ministry. If presenters want power with God, they will have to be pure before God. The Bible states:

> The LORD is far from the wicked, but He hears the prayer of the righteous (Pro 15:29).

> Behold, the LORD'S hand is not so short That it cannot save; Nor is His ear so dull That it cannot hear. But your iniquities have made a separation between you and your God, and your sins have hidden His face from you, so that He does not hear (Isa 59:1-2).

A sinful lifestyle will hinder the minister's prayers from moving the heart of God. Fasting combined with prayer further develops integrity in the life of the preacher. The late Dr. Bill Bright enumerated many benefits of fasting and prayer:

* It is a biblical way to truly humble oneself in the sight of God (Ps 35; Ezr 8:21).
* It brings revelation by the Holy Spirit of a person's true spiritual condition resulting in brokenness, repentance, and change.
* It is a crucial means for personal revival because it brings the inner workings of the Holy Spirit into play in a most unusual, powerful way.

* It helps us better understand the Word of God by making it more meaningful, vital, and practical.
* It transforms prayer into a richer and more personal experience.
* It can result in dynamic personal revival—being controlled and led by the Spirit and regaining a strong sense of spiritual determination.
* It can restore the loss of one's first love for our Lord. (Bright, 92-93)

The Results of Effective Prayer

Every minister needs to learn to pray victoriously (Jas 4:1-10). Prayer can do anything God can do, and God can do anything. Ministers need to link their lives with the God who can do anything. Jesus said, "Ask and it will be given you" (Mat 7:7), and James said, "You do not have because you do not ask" (Jas 4:2).

Every failure in the Christian life can be traced to a prayer failure. Every sin could have been prevented through prayer. Every need in life can be met through prayer.

The Presumption of Unoffered Prayer (Jas 4:1-2)

God wants to bless ministers, but the cares of full-time ministry often snuff out the life of prayer. We can feel too busy to take our cares to the Lord. Ministers often trust more in our strategies than in our supplications. We are to pray first before trying to solve problems. When ministers bring our problems, pressures, and pains first to God, we can expect to receive the solutions God has for us.

Pride is the foundation of presumption. Pride leads to sin. John Bunyan said, "Prayer will make a man cease from sin and sin will make a man cease from prayer." (Bunyan, 46) Be faithful to offer prayer.

The Problems of Unacceptable Prayer (Jas 4:3-4)

At times as ministers, we may offer prayers God will not answer. James said, "You ask and do not receive, because you ask with wrong motives, so that you may spend *it* on your pleasures" (v. 3). The Apostle James had the motive behind prayer in mind. If ministers are not careful, the motive behind some prayers will not be pleasing to God. If the desire is unbiblical, God cannot answer the prayer. Why do we pray? Do we pray for *selfish* reasons? Is it for ministerial gain? God will not sponsor selfishness or support sin.

Do we pray for *sinful* reasons? James states, "You adulteresses, do you not know that friendship with the world is hostility toward God? Therefore whoever wishes to be a friend of the world makes himself an enemy of God" (v. 4). The Church is the bride of Christ. When a Christian falls in love with the pleasures and philosophies of the world, he or she is committing spiritual adultery. If ministers are lured away by the world, their prayers will not be answered. If they are friends with the world, they become the enemy of God.

The Principles of Undeniable Prayer (Jas 4:5-10)

Do you want power in your prayers? Do you want your prayers answered? Here are five principles to undeniable prayers:

Sensitivity to the Spirit (v. 5): The Holy Spirit has some strong desires and is very envious or jealous for the total devotion of our hearts toward Christ. He wants all ministers to be completely dedicated to Christ. He does not want Jesus to have "a place" or "prominence" in our hearts but to have "preeminence." The Holy Spirit wants to lead ministers in their prayer lives. Prayer is not possible without the functioning of the Holy Spirit.

Submission to the Father (v. 6): Prayer is not a filibuster to force God to do something. The minister must submit himself or herself before God. Jesus taught this in the Garden of Gethsemane. Do you want what God wants in your ministry and life? Do you come to God with a hidden agenda or with your mind made up before you ever pray?

Standing against the devil (v. 7): Prayer is vital in the fight against the devil. There are demonic temptations in ministry. Jesus told His disciples to watch and pray lest they give in to temptation (Mt 26:41). Stand firm against the "schemes of the devil" (Eph 6:11). Flee immorality (2 Tim 2:22). Purify your thoughts (Php 4:7-8).

Separation from the world (v.8): Cleanse your hands, which means to let go of the world. Consecrate your hearts. Concentrate your thoughts on God. Worldliness has no place in evangelism. Guard your testimony. Think carefully about your words before speaking them. *Love not the world.*

Surrender to the Lord (vv. 9-10): Remorse over sin leads to repentance from sin. When a minister strays from the Lord, he or she must repent through weeping and mourning before the Lord. When the minister exemplifies true repentance, the Lord will exalt him or her in due time. The Apostle Peter wrote, "Therefore, humble yourselves, under the mighty hand of God, that He may exalt you at the proper time, casting all your anxiety on Him, because He cares for you" (1 Pe 5:6-7). This is a prayer promise from God.

The prayer promises in the Bible are for the members of the Body of Christ. Mark the prayer promises in your Bible. Memorize them. Study them. Apply them to your life and ministry. Learn to practice the prayer promises in the Word of God.

> Beloved, if our heart does not condemn us, we have confidence before God; and whatever we ask we receive from Him, because we keep His commandments and do the things that are pleasing in His sight. (1 Jn 3:21-22)
>
> This is the confidence which we have before Him, that if we ask anything according to His will, He hears us. And if we know that He hears us *in* whatever we ask, we know that we have the requests which we have asked from Him. (1 Jn 5: 14-15)
>
> Truly I say to you, whatever you bind on earth shall be bound in heaven; and whatever you loose on earth shall be loosed in heaven. Again I say to you, that if two of you agree on earth about anything that they may ask, it shall be done for them by My Father who is in heaven. For where two or three have gathered together in My name, I am there in their midst. (Mt 18:18-20)
>
> If we confess our sins, He is faithful and righteous to forgive us our sins and to cleanse us from all unrighteousness. (1 Jn 1:9)
>
> Be anxious for nothing, but in everything by prayer and supplication with thanksgiving let your requests be made known to God. (Php 4:6)
>
> If you abide in Me, and My words abide in you, ask whatever you wish, and it will be done for you. (Jn 15:7)

E. M. Bounds wrote, "Nonpraying is lawlessness, discord, and anarchy. Prayer, in the moral government of God, is as strong and far-reaching as the law of gravity in the material world, and it is as necessary as gravitation to hold things in their proper sphere and in life." (Bounds, 14)

Victorious prayer is answered prayer. The "praying prophet" Bounds also wrote:

> Prayer fills man's emptiness with God's fullness. It fills man's poverty with God's riches. It puts away man's weakness with God's strength. It banishes man's littleness with God's greatness.   Men are never nearer heaven, nearer God, never more Godlike, never in deeper sympathy and truer partnership with Jesus Christ, than when praying.
>
> Prayer is not merely a question of duty, but of salvation. Are men saved who are not men of prayer? Is not the gift, the inclination, the habit of prayer, one of the elements or characteristics of salvation? Can it be possible to be in affinity with Jesus Christ and not be prayerful? Is it possible to have the Holy Spirit and not have the spirit of prayer? Can one have the new birth and not be born to prayer? Are not the life of the Spirit and the life of prayer coordinate and consistent? Can brotherly love be in the heart which is unschooled in prayer? (Bounds, 20)

Imagine what one evangelist or pastor can do through prayer and fasting combined with the preaching of the gospel in his or her generation. Martin Luther led the Protestant Reformation. John Knox said, "Give me Scotland or I die." John Bunyan wrote *Pilgrim's Progress* from the Bedford Jail. Jonathan Edwards sparked the flames of a great spiritual awakening through his sermon, "Sinners in the Hands of An Angry God." George Whitfield, Charles Wesley, D. L. Moody, Charles G. Finney, and Billy Graham all fulfilled God's purpose for ministry to their respective generations.

Who will fulfill the role in the twenty-first century? Will it be you? Will you be known for your prayer life or your public life? Do you believe prayer is one of the greatest steps to birthing, building, and broadening a full-time, preaching ministry? This chapter serves only as a microcosm for the prayer life of the minister. The secret to successful praying is praying in secret.

Left Brain
(Principles/Rational)

Right Brain
(Pictures/Relational)

LAW

7

TRUTH MAKES A LOUSY CLUB
BUT A GREAT SWORD

He has made My mouth like a sharp sword,
In the shadow of His hand He has concealed Me;
And He has also made Me a select arrow,
He has hidden Me in His quiver. (Isa 49:2)

eople do not come to hear us speak over their heads, but to their hearts!

Reinhard Bonnke is a German missionary who has invested the majority of his ministry life in Africa. I have traveled with him and witnessed firsthand how an open field is transformed into a crammed meeting ground for hundreds of thousands of people, flocking from miles in every direction, for the opportunity to hear the great Bonnke preach.

It would be a feat for any of us to go to an open field and draw as many as two million people to hear us. It would be quite a feat to speak to a mostly unevangelized and often illiterate and superstitious crowd yet hold their interest night after night with just a microphone and some speakers. It is near miraculous that Reinhard Bonnke can do this while being true to accurate hermeneutics. Bonnke could submit the same sermons he uses in Africa to a professor in any seminary and receive the highest marks for his hermeneutics, the systematic approach by which we interpret Scripture. His evangelistic message on the woman caught in adultery is as fine a course on Christ's substitutionary atonement as any professor could even teach.

One may wonder why it would be important to study to be a fine hermeneutician in deepest Africa while speaking to people, the majority of whom may never even know the greatness of what they were hearing. One may think it is like speaking the XYZ to people who have never even heard the ABC. The truth is, every time we stand to speak for Christ and preach His gospel, we are obligated to speak from a solid foundation of hermeneutics.

There are foundational, proven processes of interpretation combined with time-tested practics of inspiration for the communication of God's Word. Gutenberg and Google leaders alike need to have a "starting point" of biblical understanding or they will simply misconnect with their audiences. It not so much how cute or creative presenters are, but how connected and communicative they are with their times.

The overarching approach of this "Law" is not a discourse on the topic nor an addition to the hundreds of works that comprise hundreds of pages per volume regarding hermeneutical principles. This "Law" is simply a brief summary of the approach that I consistently apply after having studied my way through eighty-eight seminary hours in the field of homiletics and thirty-four hours in hermeneutics.

Hermeneutics represents the left brain and homiletics the right brain. Our preaching goal is to connect both of these and deliver our message powerfully to our audience.

Over the years, I have combined hermeneutics and homiletics during the preparation of my message with the ability to connect both the right brain and left brain of my listeners. Hermeneutics represents the left brain and homiletics the right brain. Our preaching goal is to connect both of these and deliver our message powerfully to our audience. If you heard one of my presentations, you would not be able to sequentially select or find specifically these elements because they are seamlessly interwoven. The sermon is prepared to connect with the heart. Let me run through the guidelines for you briefly on the next few pages.

The preacher needs to be careful not to turn the Word of God into something that it was not intended to be. Our goal is not to beat people up with Scripture, but to allow the Holy Spirit to cut away those elements that are not Christ-like in their lives.

This has to do with what ministers believe the "inspiration of Scripture" consists of in our world today. Scripture must have the final authority in all aspects of our ministry. Our view of the Bible will determine how we preach it in the pulpit.

The meaning of the passage is achievable when all the data are researched by the minister. Preachers must keep in mind they are not called to *make* the preaching text relevant but to *show* its relevance. If Scripture is not already relevant, then the most gifted preacher cannot make it so. It is self-defeating to advocate that it is the preacher's sole responsibility to make the text relevant to today. How does the communicator make the Bible relevant to the churched and unchurched? How do ministers transfer a relevant message from Scripture to the present culture?

HISTORICAL-CULTURAL RESEARCH

Historical-cultural research focuses the preacher back to the times and events of the original writer and also compels us forward to a current sphere. To transfer the relevant message of the past to the present, the historical-cultural gap must be crossed. Since God's Word entered history in a relevant fashion, it can enter again into our world today. (Greidanus, 159) The historical-cultural gap is not crossed by al¬legorizing, spiritualizing, and moralizing the preaching text. How can the two horizons (past and present) be merged together to produce application for the listener? If we do not go down right with interpretation, we will not come up right with the parallels of application.

As preachers, we need to consistently transfer the specific message of a scriptural passage and not simply isolated parts of the pericope, the passage (Greidanus, 166). People do not want to hear every historic detail and didactic discourse of the passage. They want to hear the *message* of the passage. That is what is relevant. We are covering interpretation now, before we cover application, because before ministers can make proper application of Scripture, we must know what the original writer wanted to convey to his readers.

The grand object of grammatical and historical interpretation is to ascertain the specific usage of words as employed by an individual writer and/or as prevalent in a particular age. The most fundamental principle in grammatical-historical exposition is that words and sentences can have only one signification in one and the same connection; but many applications.

The historical sense is that sense which is demanded by a careful consideration of the time and circumstances in which the author wrote. It is the specific meaning which an author's words require when the historical context and background are taken into account.

GRAMMATICAL-SYNTACTICAL ANALYSIS

The grammatical sense is the simple, direct, plain, ordinary, and literal sense of the phrases, clauses, and sentences.

First, we must grasp the whole before attempting to dissect the individual parts of a text. Understand the total framework within which the biblical authors communicated and how that message relates to our own times. All aspects of the "hermeneutical spiral" are interwoven for the purpose of creating relevant meaning. It is the total message that contains propositional truth. The sermonizer needs to look beneath the "surface structure," the grammar, semantics, and syntax, and to the "deep structure," which is the message behind the words. Author Richard Palmer writes, "To understand a text is to understand the question behind the text, the question that called the text into being." Answering why the text was written is at the heart of interpretation in order to apply the text to the present situation.

The grammatical-syntactical analysis permits us to trace the interrelationships of the parts of the passage for its meaning and reveals the thrust of the message for the congregation. Meaning is found when words are connected together in a sentence, paragraph, chapter, or book. (Osborne, 250) We must ask and answer seven questions during the interpretation process:

1. What does the text say? Study different translations, analyze the grammar, and digest available background materials.

2. How does the text say it? Determine the genre of literature.
3. What did the text mean? See the text through the eyes of the original author and his readers.
4. What does the text mean? Attach a "zip code" or postal code to the text. Consider its literal meaning.
5. What does the text mean to me? Look through the eyes of the Holy Spirit for ourselves before preaching the gospel to others.
6. What does it mean to the congregation? Figuratively, gather the congregation around the study desk while applying the text to today's world. Anticipate objections. Turn resistance into readiness.
7. How can I make it meaningful to others? A Gospel presentation becomes meaningful through godly creativity. We must allow our imaginations to turn sermons into mirrors so people can see themselves in light of truth. Ministers are not to preach as though we are living our lives in a "protective clergy bubble" but to provide solid answers from God's Word to our world (Hull, 571).

COMMENTARIES

Sermon preparation is more than parroting the commentator's ideas and conclusions. In most instances, commentaries should be consulted *last* to test the interpretations of the immediate passage. The minister first studies the text *inductively* to protect ourselves from an uneducated reliance on commentaries. The commentator's evidence is then weighed carefully in light of the minister's exegesis of the immediate context. The context is kept in mind at every level of the hermeneutics spiral in order to proclaim a relevant biblical message.

A critical evaluation of one's presuppositions about the text is necessary because the minister brings church traditions, communal beliefs, and personal experiences to the text. Ministers must separate church traditions and dogma from Scripture. The personal experiences of the interpreter within our own communities help shape our lives and worldview. Careful sermon preparation will stop the proclaimer of God's Word from reworking the intended meaning of the text to fit personal experiences or goals. A "hermeneutic of humility" must be applied when Scripture dictates that the previous theological system or Church's doctrine needs modification or elimination. It is the continuous interaction between the text and the preacher's presuppositions that form an upward spiral to relevant truth.

Last, the interpreter "principalizes" meaning into timeless truths (Kaiser, 47). The text sets the agenda for the sermon. Grammatical-syntactical exegesis and historical-cultural background of the text reshape the minister's presuppositions. Expository preaching serves as the tool that carries ministers from a biblical concept discovered through serious exegetical study to appropriate application for the congregation.

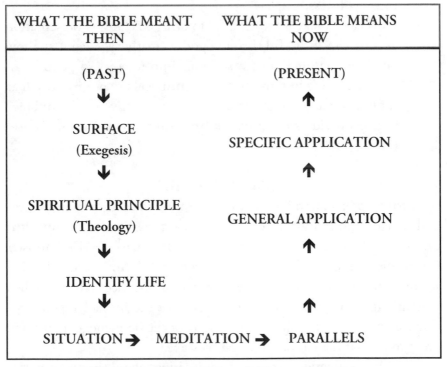

WHAT THE BIBLE MEANT THEN	WHAT THE BIBLE MEANS NOW
(PAST) ↓	(PRESENT) ↑
SURFACE (Exegesis) ↓	SPECIFIC APPLICATION ↑
SPIRITUAL PRINCIPLE (Theology) ↓	GENERAL APPLICATION ↑
IDENTIFY LIFE ↓	↑
SITUATION → MEDITATION → PARALLELS	

The Hermeneutical Spiral (Grant Osborne)

BETWEEN TWO WORLDS

Deductive and inductive reasoning are necessary to complete the bridge from an author's past meaning to relevant truth for today. Deductive study establishes the theological systems, the overall doctrines, based on scriptural evidence. Inductive study utilizes imagination to move the preacher from the theological systems to modern-day applications. An overlap between the past and present horizons is required for recontextualization (Stott, 1982).

Lively preaching paints a picture for the listener's heart. It enables the audience to see the parallels between the author's intended meaning and relevance for today. In summary, proper sermon preparation reveals past truth from the text, relates personal truth to the interpreter, and releases propositional truth for the congregation.

In the midst of our rapidly-changing culture, the preparations for evangelistic preaching are more crucial now than ever before. The Missiologist Alan Tippett has well said:

> The greatest methodological issue faced by the Christian mission in our day is how to carry out the Great Commission in a multicultural world with a gospel that is both truly Christian in content and culturally significant in form. (As quoted in Coleman, 1986, 85)

People are keener to see the gospel than to hear the gospel (Fletcher, 159). Just as Christ made people see truth through His illustrations, the effective preacher knows how to filter the interpretation of Scripture through a godly imagination in order to give an appropriate invitation for his audience to acknowledge Christ as their personal Savior.

SYNTACTICAL ANALYSIS

At the heart of exegesis, there should be a detailed syntactical analysis which involves identification of (1) the theme proposition; (2) the relationship of all other sentences, clauses, and phrases in the paragraph to that theme proposition; and (3) the connection of the paragraph with other paragraphs.

In syntactical-theological exegesis, there are two key parts of the exegetical process. The first part stresses that syntax is one of the most important avenues for the interpreter to use in reconstructing the thread of the writer's meaning. The way in which words are put together so as to form phrases, clauses, and sentences, will aid us in discovering the author's pattern of meaning.

Assuming that every word will be affected to some degree by its grammatical function in the phrase, clause, or sentence and by the words, phrases, clauses, sentences, and paragraphs which surround it, the contention of this method is that only as the exegete discovers how this surface structure works can he or she successfully begin to distinguish main assertions from supporting assertions of the text.

Syntactical analysis systemically operates from three basic building blocks: (1) the concept, (2) the proposition, and (3) the paragraph. It is through the precise way in which these three units are organized and arranged that the exegete receives all the data he or she needs to begin the journey of moving from the text to the destination of using that text in a teaching or preaching situation.

The syntactical analysis also addresses the neglected feature of theological exegesis. All too often, the exegete has had the unpleasant prospect either of delivering a message which, though based on a technically proper analysis, is but a sterile rehearsal of the words and events in a text. Or, the exegete delivers a message which imports doctrine and theological truth by the carload from all over Scripture without caring in the least whether the practice is legitimate or not. The answer is both biblical and practical balance.

Before in-depth work on a passage of Scripture can begin, it is necessary to decide what type of literary composition is before us.

Five Basic Literary Forms:
1. *Prose:* Compositions are the basic model of biblical communication.
2. *Poetry:* Poetry occupies nearly one-third of the Old Testament. Only seven Old Testament books exhibit no poetry.
3. *Historical narrative:* This is a type of prose. The key problem is relating historical truth and theological teaching.
4. *Wisdom writings:* There are two basic types:

> A *reflective type* of wisdom that tends to carry a sustained argument across a large body of text.

> A *prudential type* of wisdom consisting of smaller units of thoughts that are disconnected and often isolated contextually.

5. *Apocalyptic:* General description involves:
>   Rich symbolism
>   A formalized phraseology indicating that the revelation came
> by a vision or dream
>   Frequent conversations between the prophet and a heavenly
> being who disclosed God's secret to men
>   Cosmic catastrophes and convolutions
>   A radical transformation of nature
>   The imminent end of the present age

The Paragraph

The framework for expressing and developing a single idea is a paragraph. Once we have determined the natural divisions and the literary type(s) of the individual book, it is time to get down to examining the passage that has been selected for exegesis. How do you define the limits of a particular paragraph? How do you discern whether or not you are working with a complete paragraph? There are many characteristics of a paragraph that will help you select a portion of Scripture correctly:

1. The principal feature of a paragraph is a unifying theme.
2. Rhetorical questions will often introduce a new paragraph.
3. A vocative form of address may commence a new paragraph.
4. A sudden change(s) in the text is one of the best ways to detect the beginning of a paragraph.
5. Frequently, what appears at or near the end of one paragraph is taken up and developed more fully in the next paragraph.

We have now selected our paragraph and it is time to get down to work. Analyzing how the supporting propositions in a paragraph are related to one another is the hardest task the student, or exegete, faces. The exegete will likely be dealing most frequently with relating clauses and phrases within each sentence. The clause is a group of words which has a subject and a verb or predicate and which forms part of a sentence.

Three Types of Clauses:

1. *Independent, main, or principal clause:* Expresses a complete idea and can stand alone

2. *Coordinate clause:* Any clause that forms one part of a compound sentence
3. *Dependent clause:* Any clause which does not express a complete thought and cannot stand alone

Following are words often used to introduce various clauses:
1. *Coordinating conjunctions:* and, or, nor, for, but, yet, so, neither… nor, either…or, both…and, not only…but also
2. *Adversative coordinating conjunctions:* but, except
3. *Emphatic coordinating conjunctions:* yea, certainly, in fact
4. *Inferential coordinating conjunctives:* therefore, then, wherefore, so
5. Transitional coordinating conjunctives: and, moreover, then
6. Subordination conjunctions: when, because, if, since, although, that, where
7. Subordinating relative pronouns: who, whose, whom, which, that

The Syntactical Display

For the exegetical student to study a paragraph in terms of both its internal operation and external interrelations, I advocate the use of a syntactical display. I like to use this when studying a new text. Here is how to create one:

Each proposition, clause, and phrase is written out in the natural order of the text. Each syntactical unit is isolated on a separate line. A "theme proposition" is brought out to the left-hand or right-hand margin based upon the original language. The syntactical display shows how each word, phrase, clause, and sentence of the paragraph are interrelated to each other.

Theme Proposition: The nucleus of every paragraph is the theme or topic sentence proposition. While this sentence usually comes at the head or beginning of each paragraph, it may come in the middle or at the end of the paragraph. The theme sentence's position in the paragraph will not affect in the least its meaning or the analysis of the passage.

Independent Propositions: All of this discussion assumes there will always be only one theme or proposition and that it is always expressed. If the theme is not expressed explicitly, the interpreter abstracts the implicit theme from the several independent propositions in the paragraph. However, the exegete must make sure all of the propositions do, as a matter of fact, belong to one paragraph and are therefore closely related in topic and theme.

Transitions Between Paragraphs: Once the interpreter has mastered the analysis of an individual paragraph, the next step is to trace just as diligently the connections by which sections and paragraphs were distinguished from one another to provide the very criteria for establishing the relationship of one paragraph to another.

The best signal for a transition is a conjunction, connecting particle, or related expression. A change in the person, number, mood, or tense of the verb will also often indicate which direction the new paragraph will take. Where no connectors exist and no explicit indicators orient our thinking, the word patterns or ideas may serve as a clue to the relationships between paragraphs. Perhaps when all the paragraphs in a particular section are laid out in relation to one another, it will be clear how an apparently unrelated paragraph does, as a matter of fact, continue the development. It is just as important to observe the connections between paragraphs, especially when they belong to a particular pericope, or passage, that has been selected for exposition and proclamation, as it is to observe the connections within a paragraph.

This detailed syntactical analysis involving the theme proposition, the relationship of all other sentences, clauses, and phrases in the paragraph to that theme proposition, and the passage's connection to other paragraphs is the start of great hermeneutics. This is hard work! Yet, like anything else, with practice it can become second nature to us.

Some years ago I had a practical experience in learning the craft of good hermeneutics. One of my assignments during my doctoral studies was to translate the book of Habakkuk from the Hebrew. It just so happened that the assignment came due during a week that I was preaching each evening at a junior camp. With a few hundred excited and easily-distracted young people sitting in each evening service, I came to realize very quickly what needed to stay in my message and what needed to be removed after my study. When you have a good, solid hermeneutic, you know what you have. Then you can determine what should be kept in and what should be removed so your specific audience can grasp the message you are presenting.

It is commonly accepted that in the past, the earth's continents comprised one single land mass worldwide. Although I personally believe that the ancient biblical flood separated the land into the present continents, there is debate as to how they separated.

In the mid-1990s, the information explosion caused a rapid separation from the Gutenberg-style of preaching and the Google-style of understanding and application of truth. As a result, the style or packaging of the message from the past was for the first time hard for a younger generation to understand and to make application to everyday life. We can debate how rapidly this Information Age explosion separated the Gutenbergers and Googlers, but the fact remains, there is a huge misconnect today between those who cannot ever remember life without a computer and access to the Internet, and those who recall life when they did not use a computer and had no Internet.

It is just as hard for the Googlers to communicate to the Gutenbergers as it is for the Gutenbergers to communicate to the Googlers. This is why a sound a hermeneutic is critical to craft a rock-solid biblical understanding, even though the packaging and style may in fact be dramatically different from one audience to another.

To close this chapter, let us remember as we study that "Truth" is a living person. Jesus said, "I am the way, the truth and the life." He is not a concept but a person. Truth is not just a principle to ultimately learn, but a person to intimately love. As we strive to rightly divide the Word of God, we need to remember that the Bible was written to reveal God's Son to us. This is the truth that will set us free. Truth makes a lousy club but a great sword!

Left Brain
(Principles/Rational)

Right Brain
(Pictures/Relational)

LAW

8

THE MIND CRAVES ORDER

We are destroying speculations and every lofty thing raised up
against the knowledge of God, and we are taking every thought captive to the
obedience of Christ. (2 Co 10:5)

At the pastors conferences our ministry hosts, we often invite leaders from various parts of culture—business, the arts, government. On one such occasion, it was my privilege to interview Ben Stein, the writer, ethics professor, economist, and film-maker, among other titles. He is someone I would classify as a bona fide deep thinker. Such thinkers are usually easy to spot because they are interested in everyone and listen to everything. They enjoy crunching the data, mulling over intricate new ideas, and often form original conclusions or creative thought streams as a result. Dr. Stein was promoting a film, and his arguments for viewing it were cogent, logical, and compelling.

Some people are born with advantages. Dr. Stein, for example, is the son of a brilliant economist and attended the best schools. However, deep thinking cannot be traced to genetics, intelligence, or even training. Thinking well is not a natural gift, but the result of a disciplined mind. We can all improve our thinking. When we do, according to

Scripture, our life and ministry improves as our thinking improves. "For as he thinks within himself, so he is" (Pro 23:7).

Deep thinking cannot be traced to genetics, intelligence, or even training. Thinking well is not a natural gift, but the result of a disciplined mind.

Relating thinking to preaching, when we hear a message with no structure, we know there was not much thought given to the presentation. Our Lord brought His universe out of chaos into order. When one observes the systems of the universe, it becomes obvious that "things did not just happen," but there was a Master designer behind it all. When we stand to present the living Word of God with organized excellence, we give a positive reflection to our audience about what we believe about the Bible and the King of the Universe.

What are the foundational principles to building a dynamic ministry? Are the greatest ministries built because a leader is smarter, more gifted, or simply got the breaks in life? Is it because one did not have any problems to contend with and everything seemed to fall into place? Is it that one prays more? Is it fate? Is it the opportunities?

Imagine for a moment how your life would change if you had a guaranteed formula for ministry effectiveness. Where would your ministry be in five years? How would you change as a person? What would your contribution in life be? Following are some principles to turn your goals into reality.

The starting point to changing our life and ministry is changing our thoughts. Once the mind has been shaped by a new idea, it will never retain its original shape.

We must understand that people's minds reject what they cannot understand. People will not follow us if they cannot see the road ahead of them. God made us this way. When people come to the worship service on Sunday, they have not spent much time, if any, thinking about what we are going to preach that morning. It is therefore imperative that we come with an organized message that will capture their interest from the beginning and carry them to the conclusion.

In a previous chapter, we saw that the mind has been designed by God with a gatekeeper. It is the gatekeeper who protects that mind from danger or information that is not understood. Whether you are a Gutenberger or a Googler, your mind craves order and so does the mind of your listener!

THE MIND

The average person has tens of thousands of thoughts a day. In a 16-hour day, that amounts to roughly a thought a second. That means day in and day out, our minds are constantly whirring with impulses, notions, and urges of one sort or another in that intuitive process we call "thinking."

Obviously, any positive mental activity is good, and the more the better. As we consider our thoughts each day, how many of those thoughts are actually new thoughts? Naturally, we must have some repetition for memory's sake, but the essence of creativity and living life to the fullest is our ability to accommodate as many new thoughts as possible.

Our problem arises when we find ourselves thinking today along the same lines as yesterday, the day before, five years before, and even a generation before. Too often, we continue mulling over the same old ideas and beliefs and even dwelling on the same fears, worries, and regrets. Certainly, the very act of entertaining the same thoughts over and over again limits our capacity for new and creative thoughts. The worst-case scenario is someone's having the same thought every second of the day!

THE MOTIVATION

The goal is to leave behind old, worn-out thoughts and open our minds to new ideas, new opportunities, and new dreams. To change our life and ministry, we must change the content of our thoughts and the way we think about ourselves, our lives, our ministries, and the world around us.

This is literally the only "secret" we need to know to completely revolutionize our lives. We change the way we think. We set up a new pattern of perception that raises our awareness of the world around us and permits us to see that world more clearly. We must determine that our mission is to stretch our thought lives.

The most important foundational secret to building an effective ministry is: "Your thoughts control your life." Another way to state the meaning of these five words is: "The thoughts you choose to occupy your consciousness will control what you become." Rather than copying another ministry, we should allow other ministries to become a springboard and a sounding board for new, innovative ideas that catapult us forward into twenty-first century ministry. Our thoughts are the most powerful forces shaping our lives. Our thoughts, in fact, are among the most powerful forces in the universe.

Our thoughts have shaped our lives from childhood to the present. Unquestionably, we are where we are and what we are because of the thoughts that have dominated our minds. As for the future, our destiny is being shaped by our thoughts right at this moment. This is a most simple and challenging concept.

Yet to be of value, purposely choosing our thought life must be learned and relearned over and over. Thinking well is the kind of idea that must become ingrained in our daily consciousness. It is an elusive secret, yet it is the fundamental key to personal growth and success.

It is a wonder that something so simple can elude the majority of the earth's population. Some leaders choose to change their thinking, to control their destiny, and to build effective ministry lives while others do not. Some choose spiritual and ministerial success, and others do not. God made this "thinking principle" available to everyone, but most do not choose this path of personal growth. In fact, in North America, upon graduating from formal education, most people never read another nonfiction book.

It is critical to choose what thoughts we allow to control our lives. As ministers, we must constantly question where our thoughts are taking us. This is why simply knowing that our thoughts control our lives is such an important "secret" to personal fulfillment and ministerial effectiveness.

THE METHODS

For me, as a person and a minister, once I fully realized that my thoughts controlled my life, I also realized that my next important step was to take control of my thoughts, making every thought into a slave of Jesus Christ. This is the critical breakthrough that gives ministers the power to decide where their thoughts will take them.

What worked for me was a systematic program of thinking about the person I most wanted to become and the life I most wanted to live. Within a short period of time, I not only felt more confident and had a more positive outlook on life, but I also began to steer the life God gave me in the direction the Lord wanted me to go.

It is critical to choose what thoughts we allow to control our lives. As ministers, we must constantly question where our thoughts are taking us.

Try an interesting exercise called a "mental download." For a period of four or five days, write down everything you think about. As much as you can, keep a running list of all the thoughts that cross your mind during the day so your list represents a good cross-section of what is in your consciousness. Include all the hopes, worries, expectations, people, places, memories, or daydreams—whatever occupies your mind even for a fleeting moment. By the time you are finished, it should amount to a whole laundry list of subjects and a good inventory of the thoughts that are controlling your life.

The next step is to take a critical look at the list you have written. Ask yourself: "Are these thoughts taking me where God wants me to go?" If you conclude they are not, it is time to get your thinking on the right track.

Set aside your "mental download" list and spend the equal amount of time to make a new list. Write down the kinds of thoughts that will support where you believe God wants you to go with your life and ministry. For example, identify thoughts about ways to increase skills and capabilities. The most important tasks to accomplish each day. Ways to get along with others. Ways to improve your health. Ways to improve your communication skills. Ways to increase your service to others. Ways to increase your leadership skills. Think of as many positive directions as possible that will help you achieve what you believe God has for you and write them down.

As you write your new list, focus on the question: "What person do I admire most and would most aspire to be like?" This person may be dead or alive. Then ask: "How does that person think and act? What are his or her positive traits? In what ways does that person relate effectively to his or her ministry, family, and world?" Continue to list all the qualities you admire in that person. Once you have those good qualities in mind, begin to dwell on those qualities, think about them, practice them.

We are not talking about copying that person but discovering what makes this individual distinct, dynamic, and different. The moment we copy, we lose our uniqueness. We are also not talking about looking at what they *do* in the ministry but who they are in the ministry.

Our minds operate like heat-seeking missiles in search of targets. We are going in the direction of our most dominating thoughts. Our job is to provide the targets, meaning the right thoughts. Once we do, in a surprisingly short period of time, we acquire some of these admirable qualities for ourselves.

You cannot be completely like someone else, and you would not want to be. You are your own unique person with skills and abilities and gifts that have been reserved for you. You are here for a reason and purpose that only you can fulfill. No one else can build your ministry, your company or earn your salary, create your family, design your future, or determine your destiny. But, you can learn from others and use role models to accelerate your progress. It is not a bad idea to keep this list of positive thoughts and update it from time to time.

To be sure you never forget this idea and its power, write "My thoughts control my life" on some cards and put one in a prominent place where you will see it the first thing in the morning when you get up. Carry one with you. Keep one in your Bible. Remind yourself often throughout the day. Go through the next 30 days with this idea foremost in your mind. You will be amazed at the positive changes this process will bring to your life. This is a "secret" that will change your life: "Your thoughts control your life." You and only you can take your thoughts captive.

This is not to suggest we only think about what God wants out of our lives and never take action! That would be useless. But, the starting point of all your actions or achievements is the thoughts you hold. I promise you that the opportunities and what may seem to be serendipitous coincidences that will come your way as a result of your focused thinking will surprise you. As these changes unfold, you will rediscover this amazing secret again: Your thoughts control your life!

THE MANAGEMENT

The biggest obstacle to managing our thoughts is noise. We live in a very noisy world of traffic, crowds, machinery—loud noises that constantly assault our ears. But there is another kind of noise that can be even more disturbing. That is the noise of the information explosion, an explosion that creates a fallout of useless information—information clutter. We can become so overwhelmed by this clutter trivia, really—that we forget where we are heading in life. We forget what is important and what is not. We forget why we are here and what we really want out of life, ministry, and the future.

As bad as these distractions can be, however, there is an effective way to overcome them, focus and redirect our thoughts. Go back to the earlier list of constructive thoughts, but this time add more challenging questions. For example: Why am I here? What is the purpose of my life? What do I plan to do with my life? How can I more effectively serve God, family, church, and the world?

As difficult as these questions may seem, it is within our power to answer them. In fact, each of us is the only person who *can* answer these questions. It may take extra work, but the answers to these questions lie within us waiting for us to discover them and give them meaning. Here is one way to answer them:

To begin, find some moments to spend alone, quiet your mind, and listen to the voice of God. Imagine how you would most like to spend the rest of your life. Let your mind picture what you would love to do most—a life's work that would be most rewarding both to you and to others. Listen to that still, quiet, inner voice of God. Allow it to create a Christ-like compass for the rest of your days. Explore the interests and passions closest to your heart. Look at your talents and skills. Why did God give these to you?

The amazing part of this process is that we decide what our future will be about and what it will be like. *We* provide the answers to the questions, no one else. *We* decide what our purpose in life will be in the future. We enjoy the greatest gift in life—the Christ-centered control of our own destiny—because we control our thoughts.

We find our purpose for life by looking up to God, looking around at the world, looking inside our heart, looking behind at our past and looking ahead to our future. Our destiny is shaped by the decision we make. Once we decide, our thoughts lead us to whatever it is we want most to bring about in our lives. Controlling our own destiny means deciding to steer our lives rather than passively drifting along. As we grow as people, our mission in life grows and expands with us.

To complete this process, write down the important decisions you have made and ideas you have discovered. Fine-tune your ideas into a single sentence and memorize it. Keep in mind that you will make course-corrections along the way. You do not want to change your direction in life every day, but as you grow and develop, you will uncover new opportunities and see new possibilities come into focus. You will want to respond to change and explore new directions.

We find our purpose for life by looking up to God, looking around at the world, looking inside our heart, looking behind at our past and looking ahead to our future. Our destiny is shaped by the decision we make. Once we decide, our thoughts lead us to whatever it is we want most to bring about in our lives.

Once you are thinking along these lines, you are controlling your life with thoughts and ideas that are worthy of your time and talents. You are developing a sound intellectual framework for your life. A mind full of great ideas has no room for little ideas. It is up to you to discipline your mind to work for you instead of against you.

We do not have to know how the mind works to make it work for us. All we have to do is provide it with information, focus, and direction. The key to achieving what we want out of life lies in establishing our goals and then continuing to feed our minds with thoughts and ideas that are consistent with our goals. The Roman Emperor and philosopher, Marcus Aurelius, wrote, "Our life is what our thoughts make of it."

The Apostle Paul framed the principle for us in scripture: "Take every thought captive to the knowledge of Christ." Do that today and your life will never be the same again!

Left Brain
(Principles/Rational)

Right Brain
(Pictures/Relational)

LAW

9

WHAT LOOKS EASY IN PUBLIC
WAS HARD IN PRIVATE

And when the devil had ended all the temptation, he departed ...
And Jesus returned in the power of the Spirit into Galilee:
and there went out a fame of him through all the region
round about. (Lk 4:13-14)

uring the last summer Olympics, I was filled with a sense of wonder as one pole vaulter after another jogged into the center of the field and made it look easy to jump more than twenty feet over a bar. Amazing! My spirit soars with the deepest appreciation when I listen to a trained voice climb the scale to hit the highest notes. Inspiring! My heart kneels when I listen to a master teacher expound the Word of God. Humbling! One thing I know about each of these disciplines: Whatever looks easy in public was hard in private.

My daughter Olivia, from the Googler tribe, is taking violin lessons. Listening to her practice is music to the ears of our entire family, even if less so to her teacher. I have said to her for several years, "Olivia, as you grow older, you will hear people say, 'Practice makes perfect.' Do not believe this philosophy. It is the *right* practice that makes perfect!" Whether in violin or gymnastics lessons now, tennis or swimming later, the last thing Olivia needs to do is practice doing the wrong thing!

To master our "preaching craft," we have to know the biblical, practical, and logical rules and apply the right practice to achieve excellent results. I challenge you to make a list of who you consider to be the masters of communication today. Once you have prepared this list, make an appointment to go meet them. Take time out during your next vacation or route yourself through their city on the way to a conference. I have often said, if you have a choice between knowing the author and reading the book, go meet the author. Sometimes things are more "caught" than "taught." As your preaching ministry takes on new flavors, your impact will deepen as well.

When we "agonize the agony," we are to be willing to be stretched more so we may serve more. In the 1600s John Bunyan was sentenced to jail for preaching the Gospel. He wrote his famous book, *Pilgrim's Progress*, from Bedford Jail in London, England. While he was in prison, they threatened to starve his family. Still, he would not compromise the Word of God. His masterpiece is an allegory about a new convert named Pilgrim. The story begins when Pilgrim enters through a narrow gate and becomes a Christian. He is led to Interpreter's house to learn truths necessary for a successful spiritual journey. While in Interpreter's house he is shown the picture of a preacher. Bunyan describes the preacher as follows:

> He has eyes that were lifted to heaven. He has the best of books in his hands. He has the law of truth written upon his lips. The world was behind his back. He had a posture as if pleading with men. A crown of gold did hang over this head. (Bunyan 47)

Pilgrim had to first understand who the Preacher was and what he was called to do.

We see the graphic picture of a faithful preacher in 2 Timothy 4:1-5. To proclaim the gospel effectively, we have to understand the principles privately. Whatever looks easy on the outside was hard on the inside. Like Bunyan, Paul wrote this passage from prison:

> I solemnly charge you in the presence of God and of Christ Jesus, who is to judge the living and the dead, and by His appearing and His kingdom: preach the word; be ready in season and out of season; reprove, rebuke, exhort, with great patience and instruction.

For the time will come when they will not endure sound doctrine; but wanting to have their ears tickled, they will accumulate for themselves teachers in accordance to their own desires,
and will turn away their ears from the truth and will turn aside to myths.
But you, be sober in all things, endure hardship, do the work of an evangelist, fulfill your ministry.

These verses are inspired by the Holy Spirit and are not allegorical in nature. There are many specific commands the preacher is to follow.

Just as Pilgrim, we will step into Interpreter's house and discover how what takes place inside a person determines what takes place outside of that person. Remember that Second Timothy was to be read to the congregation. Whatever is scripturally correct for the preacher to do, the congregation must hold the preacher accountable to it. The preacher and the congregation must both conform to standards of Scripture. While the preacher is bound to the Bible, the congregation is bound to bind the preacher to Scripture.

These verses are some of the final words ever written by Paul. He was about to be beheaded for his commitment to Christ. This is in essence his last will and testament to Timothy. They are filled with emotion and a sense of urgency. To every minister of the gospel, 2 Timothy 4:1-5, reflects what a biblical preacher is to look like in the Church. When you look in the mirror of God's Word, what is the reflection that you see? It is the hard work of the private life that makes fruitful the ministry of the public life. What you are about to read represents a life of discipline that will serve you for years to come.

PREACH CONSCIENTIOUSLY

We are called to perform the commands of our commission in light of Christ's return. The first way we proclaim the Word is to *preach conscientiously in view of God's presence* (2 Tim 4:1). "I solemnly charge you…" was commonly used in court cases and legal documents. The Apostle is calling Timothy to appear in the courtroom of God's justice.

"In the presence of God" states that every minister preaches God's Word before Almighty God. In a typical trial, the judge does not know all the facts of the case. Each side tries to persuade the judge of their point of view. The presentations and cross-examinations of both sides are to assist the judge with what he does not know about the case. Yet, Christ knows everything about every detail of every human being.

The Greek word "and" that comes before "Christ Jesus" can also be translated "even." Paul charges Timothy in the presence of God, who is Christ Jesus. Scripture teaches that Jesus is the judge of the "living and the dead" (Acts 10:42; 1 Pet 4:5) and the human race (Jn 5:22; Acts 17:31; Rom 2:16; 1 Co 4:5; 2 Co 5:9-11; Rev. 20:11-15). Christ is watching everything the preacher and congregation do. Everything done in secret is at the same time done openly before God, even Christ Jesus.

In addition to preaching conscientiously in view of God's presence, we preach *in view of God's pronouncement*. "Who is to judge the living and the dead, and by his appearing and his Kingdom" dictates to the minister and his congregation the seriousness of the commission because of the One they serve and Who will judge them. The preacher is to view his ministry in light of the Second coming of Christ.

Every servant of God is directly accountable to God. The term "judge" has the idea of evaluation, not damnation. "Criteria" comes from this term. It is Christ who will evaluate our life and ministry. This judgment is for "the living and the dead." Think about this for a moment: The Christ who will judge all mankind will evaluate our ministry. Regardless of life or death, the layman and the minister will be judged for their actions. This judgment is always imminent.

This judgment will begin at Christ's "appearing." Christ's appearance upon the earth (2 Tim. 4:8; 1 Tim. 6:14; Tit 2:13). "Appearing" (*epiphaneia*) was often used in connection with the Roman emperor. When he ascended to the throne, it was called an *epiphaneia*. When he came to a town or a village and made an *epiphaneia* the people in the town or village cleaned the town before the king made his "appearance." Paul is reminding Timothy that Christ will someday make his appearance and that we need to be ready at all times.

Christ will evaluate our actions, attitudes and achievements. We will not be judged primarily for our worldly successes, but by our personal excellence before God. Worldly success is to obtain cultural goals which elevate one's importance in the culture. Personal excellence is the pursuit of quality in ones' work and effort whether the culture recognizes its accomplishment or not. Worldly success is concerned with what others think and say about us. Personal excellence is being the best I can be. Worldly success seeks to please people. Personal excellence seeks to please God. The preacher must strive to be the best he or she can be in the proclamation of God's Word in light of the appearance of Christ.

While we proclaim the Word openly, our God is judging us privately. When we are called to give an account of our lives, the evaluation that was done privately and quietly will become obvious to all.

PREACH CONTINUOUSLY

The second way the minister can perform the commands of his commission in light of Christ's return is to *preach continuously* (v.2a). We can achieve this by *fulfilling our task* (v. 5). Our task is to "preach the Word…" "Preach means to "herald or publicly announce a message." In Paul's day, a ruler had a special herald who made announcements to the people. The herald was commissioned by the king to make announce ments in a loud, clear voice so all could hear. People were to heed the message but it was not about the messenger. The Word of God is what both saints and sinners need today.

No program is an acceptable substitution in the church for the preaching of the Word. The number one responsibility of the pastor and his congregation is to make certain that the Bible is clearly articulated to everyone.

The minister is to preach like men of God in the Scriptures. Noah preached righteousness against the sin of his day (2 Pet 2:5). Jonah cried out against the sin of the city of Nineveh (Jon 3:4). John the Baptist boldly preached repentance, even to King Herod. Jesus proclaimed the truth of God.

We are to guard the sacred content of the Truth (1 Tim 6:20; 2 Tim 1:14), study the Word (2 Tim 2:15) and then proclaim it. The preacher as a herald brings God's message to men. There are many benefits from preaching the Word:

1. Gives a voice to God
2. Brings the preacher and congregation into direct contact with the mind of the Holy Spirit

3. Forces the preacher to deal with all the revelation
4. Promotes Biblical literacy
5. Crosses all cultural barriers
6. Carries the ultimate authority
7. Transforms preachers and congregations

As we preach continuously *fulfilling our task*, we will also need to *figure our time*. We are to be "ready in season and out of season." "Be ready" is a command and a military term which means "to remain at one's post whatever the circumstances." "In season and out of season" means that whether it is convenient or not, the preacher is required to proclaim the truth. There is no holiday for the preacher. No closed season on preaching. The preacher is to always have a message ready regardless of whether it is popular. The minister is not to be overly concerned with social acceptance. We are always to proclaim the truth.

Whoever said the preparation and the proclamation of the sacred message was easy did not know really what the God-given task was in the first place. Anyone who says that there is not much personal stretching to be ready in season and out of season does not truly understand what it means to consistently rightly divide the Word of Truth with the knowledge that Christ will eventually evaluate every sermon the preacher has ever proclaimed.

PREACH COMPREHENSIVELY

The third way the minister can perform the commands of his commission in light of Christ's return is to *preach comprehensively* (v. 2c-e) with the *right tone* (v. 2c-d). Preaching has both negative sides and positive sides to it. The negative aspect involves "reprove" and "rebuke." Reprove has to do with the mind. It is to biblically prove to someone that a particular teaching or act is sinful. In 2 Timothy 3:16, "reproof" has a positive ministry of teaching and instructing in righteousness and a negative ministry of correction.

"Rebuke" moves from the content of the teaching to the teacher or from the act of sin to the sinner. It has to do with the heart. It convicts the sinner of his or sin. The faithful preacher discloses the sinfulness of sin and sinfulness of the sinner.

The positive side of preaching involves the exhortation or appeal. An old rule for preaching is "He should afflict the comfortable and comfort the afflicted." Conviction without a remedy adds to people's burden.

We also are to preach comprehensively *with the right teaching* (v. 2e). The phrase "with great patience and instruction" relates to each of the previous four commands in this verse. The *manner of the minister* is found in "with great patience." The pastor needs patience because people do not change quickly and solid churches are not built overnight.

The *method of the minister* is found in "instruction." Preaching is to contain good, solid doctrine. "Rebuke" teaching provides no understanding to the solution of problems whereas instruction shows the way to recovery.

PREACH CORRECTLY

The fourth way the minister can perform the commands of his commission in light of Christ's return is to *preach correctly* (vv. 3-4) *when people lack the endurance for sound doctrine* (v. 3a). The commands of verses two and three are warranted because of the tendency of some professing believers to fall away.

"The time will come" is the third prophecy to Timothy. The first prophecy was "people will depart from the faith" (1 Tim 4:1). The second prophecy is "difficult times will come in the Church (2 Tim 3:1). The third prophecy is "people will not endure sound doctrine."

The minister must preach now because a time will come when people will not listen. "Time" means "a season or intervals." There are seasons when people will not want the truth. "Endure" means "put up with or to listen to willingly." "Sound doctrine" is connected to "instruction" in verse two. "Sound" means "healthy or clean." The English word *hygienic* comes from this term. This concept is continually emphasized in the Pastorals (1 Tim 1:10, 6:3; 2 Tim 1:13; Tit 1:9, 13, 2:8).

The preacher is not to base the success of his ministry on the size of the congregation. Today, many people lack the endurance to be faithful to church. Evangelistic meetings are in a state of decline. In some church groups, most of the parishioners are merely casual readers of the Bible. They do not hunger to mine God's Word for hidden treasure to change their lives.

We are to *preach correctly when people lust for entertainment in accordance with selfish desires* (vv. 3b-4). Paul paints the picture of a time when people will refuse to believe the truth. They have a desire against the gospel (v. 3b). They want their ears tickled. People develop itching ears. They would rather have sensationalism than sound doctrine. The gospel does not tickle the ears, but boxes and burns them.

They also have a *decision* against healthy teaching (vv. 3c-4a). "They accumulate teachers in accordance to their desires." In other words, they amass many teachers into a large pile. Teachers are handpicked for their congregation. They become the measure of who should teach them and what teaching is acceptable. These kinds of "desires" or "lusts" eventually lead them to reject the gospel.

This rejection is shown by Paul in "will turn away their ears from the truth." It is a short step from "itching ears" to turning one's ear from the truth. The faithful preacher proclaims the truth whether or not people want to hear it. These people in Paul's mind once professed to hold on to the truth (Tit 1:14). Every preacher is to communicate the Word (v.2), sound doctrine (v.3) and the truth (v. 4). The minister is often reminded to always preach the truth. The pastor is to share the truth regardless of what happens in the congregation.

The end result is their *deception* for not accepting the gospel (v. 4b). They will turn aside or become victims of myths because their minds are out of joint for rejecting the gospel. They wander away with no awareness that the truth has been left behind.

We are living in an era when people would rather have selfish entertainment than sound doctrine. Some mainline denominations are ordaining homosexuals into fulltime ministry. Christians in general are less committed to a local church. People select churches to attend based on how they feel rather than their faith. Many believers are being sucked into false cultic groups. The minister must preach now and preach correctly.

PREACH COMPLETELY

The fifth way the minister can perform the commands of his commission in light of Christ's return is to *preach completely* (v. 5a). Paul gives four commands to the young preacher, Timothy. He is challenging Timothy not to become like those who turned away from the truth (vv. 2-3). Verse five is the climax to verses one through four and the introduction to verses six through eight.

How can we preach completely? We are to preach through *thoughtful evaluation*. "Be sober" means self-controlled and stable. It is the state of mind where the minister faces all the issues with careful deliberation. The Preacher is to discipline himself in God's Word. The faithful preacher is to be careful not to quickly give an opinion on contemporary issues until there has been a "principlization" of Scripture.

In addition, we are to preach completely through *tremendous endurance* (v. 5b). There are two criteria in which to measure the preacher: 1) How much pain is he or she able to endure?; 2) How faithful is he or she to God's Word? Timothy met these two criteria. He endured hardship and was later released from prison (Heb 13:23). Preaching is not a painless exercise. I preach on average more than three hundred times per year throughout the world. Physical endurance and scriptural balance are two of the keys to effective evangelism.

If we are to preach completely, there needs to be thoughtful evaluation, tremendous endurance and tireless evangelism (v. 5c). Timothy was to evangelize even though he was not in a new and unreached city. The pastor is not to allow administration and doctrinal problems to deter from the proclamation of the good news of salvation. The work of the evangelist involves the preaching of soul-winning messages and the equipping of the saints for evangelism (Eph 4: 11).

How do we preach completely? We are to communicate the gospel through a *total effort* (v. 5d). The final command is "fulfill your ministry." We are called to fulfill all of our duties named above in this passage. These are most weighty issues. The preacher is to proclaim and apply God's Word with much patience and careful instruction. We are to remain clearheaded in every situation and bear whatever difficulties an evangelistic ministry brings.

In today's Church, we need ministers who preach completely. This is achieved through thoughtful consideration given to all points of view. Endurance is applied even if lower attendance is found in the local church. Saints are equipped to do the work of evangelism. Focus is given to who a minister is to become and what a minister is to do in order to fulfill the ministry. None of this is easy, but this divine calling takes place before the eyes of God.

When I was just beginning my evangelistic ministry, I was invited to speak at a statewide convention in the Northeast. A district official picked me up at the airport. On the way to the denomination's state headquarters, he asked me a series of questions. Knowing that I was serving as a fulltime evangelist, he said, "Do you have a singing ministry? I laughed and said, "No. You would not want to listen to me sing."

Then he asked, "Do you have a lot of exciting stores to tell in your messages?"

"No," I replied. "I am an expositor of God's Word."

"Can you make a living that way?" His question shocked me, as if these were the criteria for my preaching.

"Of course," I said, "God always provides where He guides."

I have often reflected on that conversation. Our perceptions of an evangelistic ministry were opposite. His was entertainment. Mine was exposition. His was based on stories to excite people while mine was based on Scripture to evangelize people. He was talking finances while I was acting in faithfulness to the Word of God and His call on my life.

It is time for ministers to bind themselves to Scripture and for congregations to bind ministers to the Bible. To a great degree, the Protestant Church in the West has veered off the righteous road of good, solid, biblical preaching and run into the ditch of story-telling, sensationalism, Scripture-twisting, and liberalism. Any nation's spiritual temperature will not rise higher than the spiritual temperature of the Church. The biblical consistency of the Church will not rise higher than the faithfulness of ministers. *Church attendance is only down because preaching is down.*

Let us continually take the long look into the future not just the short look today. When we are ultimately judged by our Lord, He will evaluate our lives and ministries based on private areas of our lives and what was taught to the local church. The preparation and preaching of God's Word is not an easy task. Whatever looks easy on the outside in preaching was always hard on the inside of the expositor.

Left Brain
(Principles/Rational)

Right Brain
(Pictures/Relational)

LAW

10

THE MIND IS NOT A DEBATING HALL BUT A PICTURE GALLERY

All these things Jesus spoke to the crowds in parables,
and He did not speak to them without a parable. (Mt 13:34)

esus came down the starry spangled skies of glory. He was born in Bethlehem, hidden in Egypt, raised in Nazareth, baptized in the Jordan, and tempted in the wilderness. Christ performed miracles on the roadside, healed multitudes without medicine, and charged nothing for his services. He conquered everything that came up against Him. Then, Jesus Christ took our sins up to Calvary and died for the world. He was buried in Joseph's new tomb and on schedule rose out of the grave with the power of His omnipotence.

These images in the Bible were chosen by God in order to communicate with us. Not only are the words inspired, but I believe that the images or pictures are also inspired, which the words are used simply to convey. Our challenge is to cross the past to the present so people can understand, comprehend and apply truth to their lives. We do not want to fall into the trap of thinking about what to say rather than how we should or could say it. We need biblical balance.

How do the majority of people learn? By perceiving with the right half of the brain and processing information with the left half of the brain. Word pictures connect both halves of the brain. Sermonizer

W. Macneile Dixon wrote: "The human mind is not, as philosophers would have you think, a debating hall, but a picture gallery." (As quoted in Wiersbe, 24)

In this image-rich Google world, some presenters have "bells and whistles" in their messages, yet lack real thought behind their theme or meat in their message. It's like the noise of a fire truck going by, but it has no firemen on it. There will be a lot of noise, but it won't save any lives.

The mind believes more in the images that are seen than the words that are heard. If the images do not have a biblical basis, they do not have the authority of a triune God behind them. Today's preacher serves as the filter from the text to the times and from the ancient past to the technological present. A biblical passage will generally have only one meaning, yet many applications. The meaning is biblical. The applications of it do change with the times. We cannot let go of the fact that we must be biblical, yet to be practical, we must talk the language of today's common people.

In other words, for the lack of knowing what to say, some ministers today rely on technology gadgets and film clips without much thought. Then there are those on the other side who continue to focus primarily on what to say and have not changed their style in the last fifteen years as to how to package what they are saying. The development and deployment of the Internet and computer software have shaped the way people think more than yesterday's preachers could have imagined they would.

Our God chose to communicate to humanity through Christ who was born, just as every other human is brought into this world. He chose this path to build a bridge between His world and our world so we could know Him and have eternal life. Our God knew what He was going to say and took great pains as to how He was going to say it, and show it.

Over the centuries there have been highly supplicated hermeneutical debates as to the summary image for the Old Testament and for the same in the New Testament. Many scholars believe the Old Testament pointed *toward* Jesus Christ and the New Testament pointed back to Jesus Christ. Other biblical scholars stress the Old Testament revealed "God, The Father," the New Testament revealed, "God, The Son," and today reveals, "God, The Spirit." We need not settle long-standing debates, but ask the Lord to teach us to "preach Christ effectively" regardless of the changing of culture.

Many years ago, I concluded that the center of Scripture is Jesus Christ. Jesus, the reason for the revelation of Scripture, so that all people might be saved from their sins. We are called to preach a Christ-centered gospel. Jesus is the ultimate illustration, image, picture to be fastened in the minds of your listeners. Look at the imagery associated with Jesus. His life is a treasure trove of pictures and stories that even if you preached for one thousand years, you could not mine the depths of it!

The Apostle Paul declared to the Corinthians, "For I determined to know nothing among you except Jesus Christ, and Him crucified" (1 Co 2:2). Philip preached Jesus Christ unto the Samaritans (Acts 8:5, 12) and to the Ethiopian eunuch (Acts 8:35). The Seventy preached the kingdom of God in the name of Jesus (Lk 10:9, 11, 17). Peter proclaimed "peace through Jesus Christ" to Cornelius and his household (Acts 10:36). The central thrust of the five-fold ministry of Ephesians 4:11-16 is the maturing of the body of Jesus Christ. Jesus is not simply "an issue" in evangelistic preaching but the "main issue" in the evangelistic sermon.

When the woman at the well wanted to talk about religious matters relating to the worship of God, Jesus directed her thoughts back to Himself, the Messiah (Jn 4:24-26). She came face to face with the realization that Jesus was the Son of God. He is the Christ (Jn 4:29). Evangelistic preaching crystallizes Jesus in the minds of people. "Christ should not be clouded by Christianity."

Christ is the greatest magnet in the world today. He pulls and draws people to himself as we lift Him higher and higher. It is not how cute and clever we are but how Christ-centered we are that will result in souls being saved and disciples becoming soul-winners. We cannot overrate or overstate how God chose a manner to communicate and a method so we could be forgiven and have eternal life.

The Book of Isaiah illustrates this for us. One moment, the Book of Isaiah is black with thunder and the darkness of the storm. Then, the rainbow shines through, and Isaiah sweeps his readers onto the Golden Age still ahead for the world. He writes about the Messiah as the savior and sovereign to illustrate the cross and the crown. To Isaiah, Christ is just as much the Lamb of God as He is the Lion of the tribe of Judah. This biblical passage illustrates the images that are chosen and show how these images can be preached to Googlers today. It seems appropriate that we should be reminded that twenty-seven hundred years ago, the prophet wrote Isaiah 9:6-7:

> For a child will be born to us, a son will be given to us; and the government will rest on His shoulders; and His name will be called Wonderful Counselor, Mighty God, Eternal Father, Prince of Peace. There will be no end to the increase of His government or of peace, on the throne of David and over his kingdom, to establish it and to uphold it with justice and righteousness from then on and forevermore. The zeal of the Lord of hosts will accomplish this.

The mind is not a debating hall but a picture gallery. Gutenbergers need to reach forward and bring images into their presentations and Googlers will need to reach back to make sure their messages are biblical. I have chosen Isaiah 9:6-7 to illustrate the power of combining the left brain and right brain, the information and inspiration to bring a powerful presentation.

MINISTERS NEED TO PRESENT
HIS PROFOUND PRINCIPLES

The Scriptures state that Jesus is a "wonderful counselor" (Isa 9:6). No doubt, Jesus has the answer to every question and solution for every problem. If you are *weary in mind*, Jesus says, "Come to me all who are weary and heavy-laden, and I will give you rest" (Mt 11:28). If you need basic *worldly goods*, Jesus says, "Seek first the kingdom of God and His righteousness, and all these things will be added to you" (Mt 6:33). If you are *worried about life*, Jesus says, "Take courage, it is I; do not be afraid" (Mt 14:27). If you want to be a *witness to the lost*, Jesus says, "You will receive power when the Holy Spirit has come upon you; and you shall be My witnesses" (Acts 1:8). If you are *weak in body*, Jesus says, "Get up, pick up your pallet and walk" (Jn 5:8).

Jesus Christ is the wonderful counselor. He has counsel for every crisis, a plan for every problem, a direction for every dilemma, a prescription for every pain, and a message for every man. To the Christian, the Lord's counsel is like honey to the taste, harmony to the ear, health to the body, happiness to the soul, and hope to the heart.

Please note the colorful language that I have chosen to apply in this message. The more word pictures that we can incorporate that do not conflict with each other, the greater the retention for our listeners. Additionally, you will no doubt notice that I often use rhythm, rhyming and alliteration. The point is for the presenter to incorporate as much as possible into a presentation that "pulls the message" together for the mind of the listener. The more the mind "can see" and pull together, the more listeners will understand and apply to their lives.

MINISTERS NEED TO PROCLAIM
HIS PERSONAL POWERS

Isaiah has written: "For unto us a child is born, unto us a Son is given...and His name shall be called...the mighty God" (Isa 9:6 KJV). Jesus is the God-Man. Mary knew when Jesus was born that He was older than His mother, but the same age as his Father. Before time began, Christ existed with His heavenly Father.

One of the last century's great preachers said in his most well-known message, "Christ dug deep the gorges, piled up the hills, and propped up the mountains with His will. The moon and the stars leapt on His arm. He did not have to write His signature on the corner of a sunrise because He is the creator. He did not have to place a laundry mark in the lapel of a meadow because He is the owner. He did not have to carve His initials in the side of the mountain because He is the titleholder. Christ did not have to put a brand on the cattle of a thousand hills because He is the proprietor. He did not have to take out a copyright on the songs the birds sang because Christ is the author" (S. M. Lockridge, The Lordship Of Christ, 1985).

Jesus Christ stands for free healing and full salvation. Today social scientists are able to put a new suit on man, but only Christ can put a new man in a suit. Jesus precedes all others in their priority, exceeds all others in their superiority, and succeeds all others in their finality.

MINISTERS NEED TO PREACH HIS PATERNAL PASSIONS

According to Isaiah, Jesus is the "eternal Father" (Isa 9:6). Literally, since the triune nature of God had not been revealed to Isaiah, he is expressing that Christ is Father until everlasting. Christ will still be God after eternity begins. He will be God long after the world lies in dust. He will be God when the fleeting and vaporous life we now have is gone. He will still be God when the stars leap at His command from their present orbit, and the earth melts with fervent heat from the gaze of Him whose eyes are like fire. He will still be God after all our confusions are wonderfully resolved in a heavenly understanding. He will still be God when all our weaknesses become strengths. He will still be God after our defeats become victories. He will still be God when our Sinai sojourn through the wilderness of this life gives way to the vestibule of eternity.

MINISTERS NEED TO PORTRAY HIS PRIESTLY POLICIES

Isaiah calls Jesus the "prince of peace" (Isa 9:6) and describes His domain (Isa 9:7). This passage is prophetic because it will not be fully actualized until the millennium. During the millennial reign of Christ, our Savior will rule and reign over all the earth. The *establishment* of the domain will rest upon the Lord's shoulders. The extent of this kingdom is summed up in the words of Isaiah: "There will be no end to the increase of His government or of peace" (Isa 9:7). The *expansion* of this millennial empire will materialize when Jesus is on the throne and judgment and justice are in the land.

This will be different when Jesus comes back again. The first time, He rode a donkey. The next time, He will ride a white horse. The first time, He stood before Pilate. This time, Pilate will stand before Him. At first, Jesus was rejected, but at the last, every tongue will confess that Jesus Christ is Lord. At Christ's first advent, He wore a crown of thorns. At His second, He will wear the diadems of glory. There is coming a day when Jesus Christ will make walking on water look like child's play when He steps out of eternity into time and walks on the clouds. There will be a rainbow of victory wrapped around His shoulders. There will be a smile on His face. At that moment, the laws of gravity, time, and space will simultaneously collapse and His disciples will instantly be standing on the shores of heaven. Hollywood and glitz will be replaced with holiness and godliness!

Such words illustrate the kind of picture gallery that will awaken your listeners by captivating as many of their senses as possible.

THE HOLY SPIRIT HELPS MAKE JESUS "LIVE" FOR OUR LISTENERS!

While we are preparing the message, we should pray that the Holy Spirit confirm the gospel. In Jesus' first sermon, He said:

> The Spirit of the Lord is upon me, because He anointed me to preach the gospel to the poor, He has sent me to proclaim release to the captives, and recovery of sight to the blind, to set free those who are oppressed, to proclaim the favorable year of the Lord (Lk 4:18-19).

Jesus announced to the congregation that he was "called" to preach the gospel. The Holy Spirit is the calling agent of the church and alone has the prerogative of appointing men to preach the glorious gospel of Christ. The goal of Jesus was simple: To preach the gospel effectively through the power of the Holy Spirit for the salvation of the lost.

The Holy Spirit has a three-fold strategic role in the sermon preparation. First, the Holy Spirit is the "producer," or inspiration, of the Word of God (2 Tim 3:16-17; 2 Pe 1:20-21). Second, the Holy Spirit is the "penetrator" of the man of God. The Holy Spirit opens the mind, illuminates the evangelist so proper interpretation and application can be made to the people. Third, the Holy Spirit is the "provider" of the preacher's authority during the actual preaching of the gospel. There can be no doubt that the Holy Spirit confirmed the message and ministry of Jesus Christ. The gospels are filled with recorded miracles and transformed lives. Without the conscious anointing of the Holy Spirit upon the life and ministry of the minister, there will be no long-lasting fruit in the local church.

The end result of a salvation sermon is not decisions for Christ but disciples for Christ. We are not just loggers cutting down trees but craftsmen designing furniture out of the wood. The end result of the soul-winning message is "changed lives."

Our preaching should ultimately produce evangelists who will carry the gospel to their respective people groups. This concept is often neglected in traditional homiletical textbooks. The task of the communicator is not to impress people, but to impact them; not just to convince them, but to change them. In John 4:39, Jesus Christ knew the most effective way to reach Samaritans was to have a Samaritan become an evangelist. New Testament preaching does more than produce a "great moment of evangelism." It fosters a "great movement of evangelism" (Hutchcraft, 65).

Success requires a successor! Are we focusing on what we produce or what we reproduce? Is our preaching ministry leaving behind an army of evangelizers in the local church and community?

When I was just twelve years old, I would sit on the front of Evangel Assembly in Montgomery, Alabama, with pen and paper to take notes of the sermon. Throughout my teen years, I continued to do the same, even when our family moved to another church in Mobile, Alabama. During those important, formative years, I was fortunate to hear creative expositors preach the Word of God. When the Lord called me to "preach the gospel," I accepted His divine call and never ran from it.

Even though decades have come and gone, I have often reflected over messages that I heard preached in my youth. My pastors through those years had an indescribable impact upon my life, my thinking about Scripture, and how to proclaim the Gospel. When I returned home from Bible College, and later, seminary, I was privileged on numerous occasions to preach in my former home churches. Those were sacred days, months, and years.

Maybe you have just begun your preaching ministry or you could have been preaching for decades. There is never an end to the need for effective role models that challenge us to grow in our ability to communicate the greatest message ever written or told to any generation. When we study the messages and sermons in the Bible, we find not only insights and truths, but we learn methods applied then that have significant impact on our ministry today.

So much of future growth and our ability to weather the storms of life is to know without a doubt we have been called to "preach the gospel." Think about Jesus' statement for a moment. He said, "The

Lord has anointed me to preach." The very Son of God was called and anointed to deliver a life-changing message in the synagogue. Even more so, we must be able walk through and live out God's divine call upon our lives. Our Lord is still calling Gutenbergers and Googlers to present, proclaim, preach and portray the Gospel to this generation. To whom the Lord calls into fulltime ministry, He equips to fulfill the God-given task for our times today.

While preparing the message, coincide practical ways the listeners can live out what you are communicating to them. If our messages seem unrealistic, then we will find our listeners becoming defensive to the gospel. At times we have to preach from texts that our audience may not want to hear. In those situations, we can still build bridges and bring our audience closer to the truths being taught and make them memorable. Is it not time for the minister to preach like Jesus?

Recently a well-known pastor in North America wrote an article about preaching in a major magazine. He stated that we should not preach on sheep and shepherds any longer since our culture no longer understands the concept. Yet, we do not have the authority to pick and choose what passages are relevant and what passages are not. If we are not permitted to preach on sheep and shepherds, then think of all the pericopes that we will not be able to communicate any longer. We will not be able to preach from Psalm 23 or even from the very words of Jesus when He speaks of sheep and shepherds. What about the birth of Jesus when the shepherds came to see Him? It is our God-given responsibility to preach the entirety of Scripture. The Word of God makes a lousy club but a great sword!

Left Brain
(Principles/Rational)

Right Brain
(Pictures/Relational)

LAW

LENGTH IS NOT DETERMINED BY THE CLOCK BUT BY THE CROWD

And every day, in the temple and from house to house, they kept right on teaching and preaching Jesus as the Christ. (Acts 5:42)

More than fifteen years ago, I was beginning a series of meetings in Newark, New Jersey on a holiday weekend. The church started the meetings with a long musical program which minimized the focus of the evangelistic message. When the pastor went to the pulpit to introduce me, it was 11:50 a.m. and the services were to conclude shortly after noon. I could have thought, "These people better pay attention and no one better move until I finish my masterpiece of a sermon."

The pastor then introduced me saying, "The first time I met our speaker today was in my office this morning. He comes from the Midwest. Please help me to welcome him."

Since the people did not know me and did not know anything about our ministry, I was facing an uphill battle to gain the attention and respect of the audience. I walked to the pulpit, thanked the pastor, and said, "It is my honor to be with you today. I just noticed on my watch that it is 11:50 a.m. It is amazing how quickly time passes in a worship service. Please look at your watch with me. If you will give me the opportunity to minister to 12:20, I promise to finish by that time.

In a moment, however, when I request us to stand for the reading of the Scripture, if you must go, then feel free to be dismissed."

When the audience stood, only eight people left the service. What did I accomplish in two or three minutes with an audience who had never heard me minister before? I immediately built an emotional, trust-worthy bridge to them that said, "I recognize the hour and will respect your most precious commodity: your time!"

We began our evangelistic services that morning, and they became some of the best I have ever conducted in my twenty-five years of minis-try. The length of the sermon is not determined by the clock, but by the crowd.

There are no doubt speakers you have heard that have gone too long, while others have gone too short. There are those times we have said, "Will this person ever end?" Other times, we have said, "This leader finished too soon. I wish I could have heard more." What is the secret to becoming the presenter that people want to hear more instead of less?

It is important we know our surroundings and understand our audi-ence at all times during the preaching of the sermon. This is crucial to effectiveness. A sermon is not too long because the clock says so. It is too long if the audience says so. If you are wondering if the people are following you, walk to the outskirts of the platform and watch the heads of the people. If their heads turn as you walk, they are with you. However, if the people refuse to follow you, you need to conclude the sermon as quickly as possible.

The shorter the time left in any setting, the more the people must be convinced of the importance of the presenter or the presentation. This holds true regardless if you are the presenter or the one to introduce an invited guest. It is unfortunate but true; we live in a clock-centered instead of a compass-lead culture. *The bigger the "why" you give the people, the longer the attention span.*

Because "master time" is often dictating the thinking of people, we must reflect over it, redeem it and release it.

Reflect Over Time
Regardless of our wealth, no one has been given any extra minutes in any given day. Often, time is wasted during a worship service simply

because the leader does not value time like he or she should. When every moment is given proper reflection before the event takes place, we are more apt to be successful with our desired outcomes. We are to squeeze all of the life out of each day in general and each presentation as well. If we do not respect "father time" then we will fail in the organization and preparation for each presentation of the gospel to our audience.

The shorter the time left in any setting, the more the people must be convinced of the importance of the presenter or the presentation.

During your reflection, secure copies of different worship schedules. Observe how leading pastors organize the worship service. Discover how much time they allot to the presentation of the gospel. Sometimes, just one new idea will spark fresh creativity in your mind and heart—the mind being the practics and the heart being the passion. We need both practics and passion to navigate successfully the ebbs and flows of presentation opportunities.

The deeper one thinks through the issues, the freer he or she becomes. The person who says, "The Holy Spirit will lead us," or, "The Holy Spirit will fill our mouths" is often the same person who has not carved out time to reflect over the causes, choices and consequences of people who do not listen to his or her message. People are more apt to give their money than to give their time. The cause has an effect, the choice has a chain and the consequence has an eternity!

The Weekly Task of Time

Each presenter needs to develop a sense of time needed for the average message. For example, most of my messages are between forty to forty-five minutes. Yet, there are numerous instances each year when these messages are shortened for various reasons. The overarching point is that if you do not cultivate a sense of how much time is normally needed, you will find yourself over-preparing and trimming your presentation as you present each week, even though other stage participants have been respectful of time.

A good rule of thumb is that approximately eight hours is needed to prepare about a forty-minute message. Once the presenter has come to understand the average amount of time needed each week, then he or she can effectively reflect over time, redeem time, and release time for powerful results.

Be sure to study what the Bible has to say about time. The Scripture was given long before the invention of the clock, yet the Lord has a timeline and a prophetic schedule. Our Lord operates above and beyond time, yet He also orchestrates and organizes in the world of time. Of course, we are not to become slaves to "father time," but we need to learn to respect time if we are to truly appreciate each and every day.

Redeem The Use Of Time

We also need to *redeem time* "for the days are evil" (Eph. 5:16). When it comes to the presentation or the worship service, when moments are lost, time must be redeemed. Most of the time, it is the sermon that is sacrificed due to poor management at another juncture in the service. It is usually the minister who has to adjust his message, or the guest speaker who is placed in a predicament due to wasted time earlier in the service.

The overarching reason for this common outcome is that many other activities are valued more than the preaching of the Word of God. If we were to take a poll, we spend more time thinking about the announcements, the music, the offering, and less time on how to protect the sacred time of the presentation of the Gospel. The preaching of the Word is the time when God speaks to His people. Due to the Christian tradition that I was raised in, I have often heard, "The Holy Spirit really moved today and we did not even hear a sermon." I look forward to the day I hear, "The Holy Spirit really moved today and we did not even have singing, announcements, and offering; we just preached the Word!"

We need to *redeem time* in general and the "preached Word" in particular. If people are going to be turned back to God's Word, then we must reevaluate its placement, priority, and purpose. All of us have been in worship services when someone chose to sing too long, share announcements without time consideration, or other surprises that we were not counting on that day. So, how do we redeem the time?

Process in Place

First, as leaders we should have a *process in place* with our team so these are not common occurrences. If the process is bad, the product will be bad. There is a process of success in every stream of society. We should incorporate the necessary checks and balances during the week so maximum results are obtained each weekend. Many pastoral teams meet each week to assess the previous weekend so they can eliminate past mistakes and continue to incorporate those elements of effectiveness into future worship services.

Plan to Practice

Second, as preachers or presenters of God's Word, we *need to know our message* so well that we can adjust the sails so we are successful with our sermon. I do not memorize my sermon, but I mentally organize my sermon. This organization brings great freedom to me when I am not given ample time.

Many years ago, while preaching in Memphis, Tennessee, the pastor leaned over to whisper when a person chose to spend more time talking about her special song than actually singing it. He said, "Do you know what Psalm 151 says?"

"No, I don't know what Psalm 151 says," I whispered back.

"It says, blessed is he that preaches but does not sing, and blessed is he who sings but does not preach."

The point was and is, each of the stage participants has a role. They need to understand what the roles are and what the goals are for the service.

When I find myself in a situation where time has not been respected and the preacher's task has not been redeemed, I begin thinking through the most sacred elements of the message. Immediately, my mind moves from the good highlights to be spoken, to the best thoughts to be shared in that setting. For example, normally I have at least one illustration for each main division of the message. I begin assessing which illustration could be eliminated without closing the windows to the soul. Illustrations are there to illustrate. They are the windows of a beautiful home. They let the light into the mind and heart.

Once I have mentally eliminated one illustration or story, then my mind goes to the introduction. I think of the shortest yet most creative way to introduce the message so people will get into the message as fast as possible. The reason for this is because the audience at this moment is thinking about the "tiredness of time" and wondering how late the worship service is going to go. By my getting them quickly into the message, their imagination is captured sooner, and they are more likely to go with me to the end. If we ignore this at the beginning, most people will mentally check out before we ever have time to engage their senses.

Once I have thought through the illustrations and introduction, if I still believe more time is needed to be redeemed, then I will choose not to lead in oral prayer before my message begins. One of our public traditions is to pray after the Scripture is read, followed by preaching the message. However, if time is extremely short, I will pray quietly in my heart before going to the pulpit, offering the message to my Lord.

I am sure that you can think of creative and dynamic ways to redeem the time when needed. With experience comes a variety of mental methods to recapture lost time so we can be effective. One of the greatest expositors of the twentieth century, Dr. Stephen F. Olford, had a biblical process that he applied for many decades. Before he would preach, he would repent, reflect, and recommit his life. The point being made here is that each of us needs to have a pattern or a path so we can carve as much "think time" out of our lives as possible, to reach our personal and professional potential.

Release Of Time

We also *release time.* What do I mean by this? We can either choose to use time or lose time. We cannot take time, borrow time, or give time. We can either embrace it or be embarrassed by it.

A long-term pastor has a huge advantage that a guest presenter very seldom has. The deeper the emotional equity or higher the trust factor, the greater flexibility he or she has before the hearers. In other words, most people have a higher level of forgiveness or tolerance with those who successfully preach the Word for many years. The greater the respect, the more release of time. When we consistently respect the time of our listeners, then they will release us when the service goes longer than normal.

When a pastor has a guest presenter, he or she should give the guest as much time as possible. Yet, if for some reason time is not redeemed, the pastor must instruct the congregation as to the importance of carefully listening to the guest presenter. It is at that precise moment that a powerful introduction must be given to arouse the audience to focus on the presenter that is about to bring a message. These few moments will redeem more time in the minds of the listeners and will release the presenter on a higher level of respect. The pastor who ignores this makes it doubly hard for the guest to gain proper attention.

Having said this, however, if you are the guest, all hope is not gone. If time has not been redeemed prior to beginning your presentation, determine your message length based upon the normal dismissal time. Then, simply walk to the lectern, acknowledge the time, apologize for the lateness of the hour, and quickly redeem the time. Once you have convinced your audience that you know the time and that you will shorten your message, people will relax, and time will be released in your favor. To ignore this in a clock-centered culture will cause one to hit a foul ball instead of a single or a home run.

Dr. Ademola Ishola serves at the General Secretary of the Nigeria Baptist Convention in Lagos, Nigeria. As I write today, more than ten thousand Nigerian Baptist churches are flourishing. Dr. Ishola and I serve together in the Billion Soul Network to challenge the global Church to double in size in this generation. In September 2007, I flew more than 15,000 miles to Nigeria and was driven to Bowen Seminary in Ibadan, Nigeria, for a twenty-minute presentation. Upon my arrival, I watched Dr. Ishola begin making time in the schedule so I could have as much time as possible to present the Billion Soul vision to his pastors and distinguished leaders. I arrived late in the afternoon, but his introduction awakened the audience. I noticed that they were listening with deep attention.

When I came to the platform to speak to the audience, I could sense energy among the listeners. They were ready to listen. In just a matter of moments, Dr. Ishola had awakened the audience and set the stage for me to deliver a powerful twenty-minute presentation to motivate key leaders to synergize their efforts for the fulfillment of the Great Commission.

Due to the high respect that the leaders had for Dr. Ishola, he was able to release enough time for me to share in the middle of the afternoon.

In spring of 2009, I traveled as a guest to several denominational ministers' conferences to motivate pastors to go out and help redeem the world. At one, the district superintendent brought a video presentation on church planting. The video presentation was cheaply done, lacked excellence, and was far too long, running nearly fifteen minutes. A video is considered too long at eight minutes, about right at four minutes. It was already late in the evening, so about three minutes into the video, I could see that most of the audience had mentally checked out. Upon the video's end, the leader proceeded to continue speaking of the need for church planting and challenged the people to give a generous offering toward the effort. I do not know what the offering was, but I am certain it was not a record amount!

In this instance, it would have far better to make this presentation much shorter in order to gain the attention of the audience. When a presenter does not know his or her audience and does not have a sense of timing, he or she will cause a misconnect with his audience. We need to remember that the length of a presentation is not determined by the clock but by the crowd.

Left Brain
(Principles/Rational)

Right Brain
(Pictures/Relational)

LAW

12

FAILURE IS NOT IN LOGISTICS BUT IN NOT KNOWING THE AUDIENCE

Seeing the people, He felt compassion for them,
because they were distressed and dispirited like sheep
without a shepherd. (Matt 9:36)

or close to fifteen years my wife, Sheri, and I traveled together in ministry. Today she home schools our children while I continue to preach. During those years, our life on the road was a well-oiled machine. We would leave home on the next-to-last flight on Saturday, eat with the pastor when we landed, preach Sunday morning, nap Sunday afternoon, minister each night, work each day, then head for home on the first flight back on Thursday morning. Week in and week out. I had been ministering in a different church every week for four years before we married, so this was simply the only life we knew. On occasion, however, we would experience a slip up.

After a particularly exhausting week, we fell into one of those deep Sunday afternoon naps. We awakened at 6:20 p.m. and, through groggy minds, realized the evening service had begun at 6:00 p.m.! Panic set in as we flew around the hotel room getting dressed. I had no time to prepare or reflect on my message. If I did not know it, it was far too late to get ready now. We rushed out of the hotel and arrived at the church just in time to go straight to the pulpit to minister the Word. This is when I learned the value of what I call "knowing your message cold." Even though the burden has not left you, you know your message so well that you are ready to preach it even when life throws a curve ball at you.

You can imagine the many scenarios we have weathered over the decades of itinerate preaching. For every minister, circumstances are sometimes beyond our control. The electricity can go out, the air conditioning fail, the DVD can freeze, and even babies can cry. Yet, the polished presenter learns how to turn what seems negative into positive ways to communicate the gospel. *We need to know our presentations cold and not just hot.*

Sometimes after a sermon does not go as planned, a presenter will fault the wrong thing or the wrong person. There is "power in the pause" when unforeseen problems come to our presentation. We have to pause and think of the people who are watching us, our audience, in order to succeed despite the hiccups. I have heard preachers say some unkind things from the pulpit. You can dress like you are intelligent, but everyone will know the truth when you open your mouth! If you know the message but do not understand your audience, then you can still fail in your presentation.

To learn how to see your "people" and know your audience in order to generate a favorable response, keep these principles in mind:
- Purpose of the presentation is to persuade.
- Perceptions are more powerful than facts.
- People are inundated with information.
- Problem of forgetfulness is pandemic.

THE PURPOSE OF THE PRESENTATION IS TO PERSUADE

Ministers often act like we are the exceptions to general rules. But, in the case of public speaking, most people forget what the presenter has to say faster than the presenter could ever know. We are not exempt. We spend a great amount of time preparing and presenting although most of the time, people are not persuaded and remain unchanged. Effective presentations are balanced and satisfy four basic criteria: they are attention-getting, meaningful, memorable, and activating.

If our presentations do not persuade people, there is no reason for so much effort. Why prepare and invest so much time if we are not going to achieve much result? Think about this. What is the total earnings of the audience to whom you are speaking? The speaker and the audience represent a large investment of time. It may surprise you to calculate how much is lost when a presentation is unproductive. In other words, why invest so much time and money if we are not going to persuade people to become involved in our effort? If we are not going to reap, then why sow the same way week after week and year after year?

The audience may not realize what is happening or know what your goal is "deep inside your heart," but the bottom line of your presentation is not simply to convince people but to end up with new converts. Your goal is to persuade the listeners that you really do know what you are talking about and that you have come to right conclusion. (Arredondo, 4).

The audience responds as the presenter intends when the presenter attends to the audience. Persuasive presenters follow the rules of the road, the proven principles, and targeted techniques. Persuasive presenters recognize that speaking is intended for the benefit of the listener. There's no better way to persuade people than to give them what they perceive they need in their lives (Arredondo, 5). If every preacher approached the presentation from the perspective of persuading, there would be many more effective preachers and many more people coming to Christ.

THE PERCEPTION IS MORE POWERFUL THAN FACTS
Public-speaking author Lani Arredondo, states:

How an audience perceives a presenter can persuade them to, or dissuade them from, listening and responding. What the audience perceives to be true carries more weight than what is actually true . Presenters who create positive perceptions generate opportunities and results. Presenters who are unaware of or unconcerned with how they are perceived risk having little influence on an audience or influencing them in a way they don't intend . Perceptions are formed on three different levels. Like computers, our minds (1) receive input and (2) process it. Unlike a computer, we then (3) make judgments in the context of our experience. While there's not much you can do about your listener's previous experiences, there's a great deal you can do to shape the ones they're having with you and what they will perceive when you preach or present (Arredondo, 4-5).

A presentation isn't confined just to what you say or what the audience hears. The audience responds based on what they receive through all their senses. Remember, when you present, they receive through what you say verbally, how you sound vocally, and how it all looks visually. People are affected by the entire presentation and not just a portion of it.

Here are some questions for you to ponder. Does your audience have sufficient interest in your topic or in how you're presenting it? If not, how can you create a greater interest in this subject? Do they have a need for the information, or are you creating a need? Have they had negative experiences about this subject in the past? Will these experiences hinder them from believing in what you have to say or teach? These questions and more like them should be considered carefully. Take some time to reflect and write down your thoughts before your next presentation in relation to your audience.

How People Process Information
In the same general process that we enter and retrieve data and information from our computer, people process new information in the same manner. Without a program that ensures conformance to standards of data entry and organization, input errors result in processing errors. When we do not understand how a program functions, then we will waste time and the applications will not be successful. These same principles and practices can easily be applied to our audience. It is critical that we understand people and know how they process information and apply it to their lives.

You communicate the words, phrases and paragraphs of your message into the context of a person's mind. As the presenter, you are responsible to make sure what is in your mind is safely placed in your listener's mind. You know the points that are going to follow the point that you're making now; but members of the audience not only do not know what you are doing to say but do not know the logical sequence you plan to choose to communicate to them. They come to your presentation cold without spending much time thinking about it. Your audience will try to listen and to figure out what your presentation is about, but they will not try very hard. It is the responsibility of the presenter to connect the right and left brains of listeners so they will really understand and accept what you are teaching them. Gutenbergers want firm facts and Googlers want fast facts. At any rate, we must understand how people process information if we wish to inspire them to make the changes necessary.

Most people are not trained to listen well. People will not put their minds to the task of organizing your message if the task is a strenuous one. If the input they receive is complicated, cluttered, or unorganized, the average persons will tune out. They will say to themselves, "If this presentation is so important, then why didn't the presenter do a better job organizing it?" The overriding perception that will form in the mind is that the presenter does not even know what he or she is talking about or the presentation would have been clearer. Not only is the attention span shorter for Googlers, but their patience is shorter also.

Arredondo states:

> Audiences will not do the organizing for you. You have to do it for you, and you have to do it for them. It is, after all, your presentation. They'll perceive it in a more positive light if you make their job as listeners easy. That means well organizing the content of your message. It means eliminating distractions from the environment. It means using appropriate audiovisuals. It means doing all you can to minimize data entry and processing errors. This will increase the chances that the audience will perceive what you've presented in the way you intended (Arredondo, 6).

How People Reach Conclusions

The second factor in the perception process is a natural outcome of the previous one. Having received and processed what's presented, people in the audiences evaluate the experience. They will form subjective opinions. They judge a presentation on the basis of how meaningful it was for them or how did the message make them feel. If they think the presenter is unbelievable, then they will be suspicious of all the content that was shared with them. Most people will dismiss what they have heard if "it does not feel right" to them.

"In many respects, presenting is an art. The whole room is your canvas. The facts are the fibers of your paintbrush. Brush strokes alone do not make a masterpiece. It's how the brush strokes are applied. Through the artful combination of all the elements of presenting, you create a product people perceive to be of value" (Arredondo, 7). With the advancement of technology, many more options are available to presenters today. We should strive to incorporate as many as possible, without becoming a "circus of lights and sounds" that lacks meaningful content to give to our valuable listeners.

There aren't enough facts in a set of encyclopedias to recoup what a speaker loses when the audience sizes them up one way and their presentation information is the opposite of what people perceive them to be. The next time you prepare to present, ask yourself: How do I want to be perceived by my listeners? What are the first thoughts I want my listeners to think about when I begin my presentation?

THE PEOPLE ARE INUNDATED WITH INFORMATION

In today's proliferation of information, it is estimated that the average American receives thousands of verbal and visual messages a day. With the combined amount of television that the average person views and the amount of time he or she uses other electronics, one can easily conclude that people are baptized in information as never before.

Understanding this ought to cause us to reflect. The people we address in presentations are victims of this information explosion. In every audience are people who are swamped with information and have fallen behind at work or about to give up. For you, the presenter, this means you are competing for people's attention every time you bring a sermon or a message to them. People come to our presentations with a lot of things on their mind, a lot of information they are already trying to absorb at work and in their home. Behind every smiling face is a story of victory or defeat. If we have the opportunity to present a theme or subject in the form of a series, we then can gradually provide the needed information in smaller amounts to overloaded people. As Stephen Olford used to say, "Give God-sized vision is bite-sized pieces."

"Even the most skilled presenters know that they never have everyone's full attention…. The moment that the momentum of a presentation drags, people's mind will wander. Mentally, they go off elsewhere. All kinds of things occupy people's thoughts. Having people's attendance does not guarantee that you have their attention" (Arredondo, 8-9).

Presentations that just heap on information will be no more than grist for the mill. Our messages have to do more than simply inform;

they have to first impact us and then be able to impact them. Our goal is to activate, not just motivate. If you really believe your message is important to you and you want to make it important to them, you will become an excellent presenter. This does not mean that you have to be naturally good. If this was the case, then I would have never succeeded. The majority of us have to learn how to present. We have to know how to prepare, package and deliver the message we want people to accept.

Remember, you do not need to tell people everything you know. Present only what they need to hear to be persuaded to accept your message.

THE PROBLEM OF FORGETFULNESS IS PANDEMIC

Please remember that your listeners cannot remember fifteen sermons that you have preached in the last year. I realize that this may sound disappointing, but we need to understand that people forget fast because of information overload. Our brains are like an electrical circuit box. When the circuits are overloaded, they shut down, and the house will get dark. We need to make sure that our applications in our message come fast on the heels of interpretation and information or the lights will go out in your listener's mind. It is estimated that only two people out of ten will remember what you had to say during a presentation.

The good news, however, is that effective presenters are perceived to be different. When you are perceived as knowing what you are talking about or being truly qualified to give the presentation, the retention percentage increases rapidly (Arredondo, 10-11).

> *People come to our presentations with a lot of things on their mind, a lot of information they are already trying to absorb at work and in their home. Behind every smiling face is a story of victory or defeat. If we have the opportunity to present a theme or subject in the form of a series, we then can gradually provide the needed information in smaller amounts to overloaded people. As Stephen Olford used to say, "Give God-sized vision is bite-sized pieces."*

The Four Basic Criteria of Effective Presentations

The spoken language takes on greater meaning when we clothe it in visual imagery. Googlers will be more engaged when pictures and principles are connected during the presentation. Poets have understood this for centuries. Presenting is a balancing act. On one side are relational elements and the other side rational. Lean too far one way or the other, and the results are less than effective.

Attention: Whenever you are preparing to present, ask yourself, What will get and keep this audience's attention? How can I make my message more meaningful and memorable for them? What will move them to act on what I present? Do I have enough influence, or do I need at times the assistance of others?

An effective presentation gets and keeps attention. It is meaningful and memorable for the audience. It moves people to act on the message they've received. An effective presenter aims at increasing understanding and influencing the way people think, feel, and behave. It stands to reason that when we have maintained people's attention and presented a message that is meaningful and memorable for them, they will be more inclined to act on it in response.

Activate: The minister is called by God not merely to motivate the audience but also to activate them. Motivational speeches abound. But measurements of people's galvanic skin responses show that motivation is typically short lived. (Decker, 47) It has long been proven that the human body has more electricity in it after a good motivational speech. But, what happens when a person returns to the "real world"? The electricity weakens, and most people do not follow through on their commitment. As the energy levels drops, most people fail to follow through on their commitments (Arredondo, 11-14).

When presenters demonstrate that they know who they are speaking to, the audience is appreciative and respective. Knowing your audience is a precursor to selecting the best approach to your subject. Even though you may give the same presentation or message more than once, it is imperative that you still know your audience. The wise presenter does not give the same message the same way to different audiences. When we have done our homework, we will know our audience and be more apt to be successful with them.

There are many simple ways to let your audience know that you understand who they are and know who you are speaking to. When presenting, you can call someone's name to demonstrate that you are speaking to them on a personal level. You can use terms like, "For managers like yourselves..." or "Spiritual leaders like you...." When these kinds of expressions are used the presenter is demonstrating that he or she knows to whom they are speaking.

The minister is called by God not merely to motivate the audience but also to activate them.

Choose your subject matter and the level that this subject is going to be presented. This demonstrates that you know who you are speaking to. Over the years, I have watched presenters walk up to a podium and begin presenting with information that is either above the understanding of the audience or below where the audience has already been in their training. Either way, the audience is insulted due to the lack of respect to them.

There are times when the basics of any profession need to be taught again, even to the so-called experts. But, to do so without telling them in advance is to hit a foul ball. The opportunity exists to hit a home run on every occasion. I am sure that some pastors may wonder why I ask so many questions before I speak for the congregation. My goal is to hit the target in people's mind when I stand up to bring a presentation. It is a waste of time to fly across the nation or to a remote place in the world and assume that my presentation will fit, regardless of to whom I am speaking.

Application: What will entice people to pay attention to my message? What will activate them to carry out my objective? Most of us are motivated by self-interest. We respond on the basis of what things mean to us. Effective presenters never fail to relate a message in terms of how it applies to the audience. People come to our presentations listening to, WIFM (**W**hat **i**s in it **f**or **m**e?) This sounds self-centered, but remember how Jesus preached. He studied the needs of the people, and He knew and understood that the people's thoughts were centered primarily on their needs, even when they were in the presence of the Son of God, Savior of the world, promised Messiah.

The term "application" has two meanings: (1) how the information could possibly be applied by the audience while they hear the presentation and (2) how the presenter applies the message to them. What we want to consider here is how to apply your message to people in a way that appeals to their zip code or where they live and work. They must be able to see these valuable results immediately or they will lose interest fast.

The answer is value. When people perceive value in a product, they are far more likely to buy it. Similarly, when an audience perceives there is value in your ideas or in your message, they will be far more likely to listen, accept, and act on them. Even the title of your presentation will determine whether they will listen to what you want to teach or whether they even want to attend your presentation. We communicate with every word we write or speak.

The more specific you are in your applications, the more your audience will enjoy your message and will listen to you longer. Please do not leave it up to the audience to figure out the value of the presentation. Tell them specifically how this will benefit them.

Attraction: When you begin a presentation, there is a distance between you and the audience. The goal of the presenter is to create an attraction between your listeners and you and to close this gap as fast as possible. You are before the people, and people are before you. They have no idea what you are going to do. Personalizing your presentation creates an attraction and closes the gap that initially exists between you and your listener. It is your responsibility to convince your audience that you are approachable.

Personalizing your presentation will close the gap and make you more successful with your audience. Closing the gap means involving the audience in the message by making them feel that you are walking with them, even though you may have some insights that they do not know yet or have done yet. In other words, you are walking with them, but a few steps ahead of them.

The foundation of this law, *failure is not in logistics but in not knowing the audience,* prepares us for law thirteen, *if we speak offensively, people will respond defensively.* It is not either/or but both/and for the presenter to be successful. These two laws are like a handshake, one being informational and the other relational. I have come to understand over the years, people must feel comfortable with me before they will be confident in me. The higher the confidence level the higher the commitment level to the content of the presentation.

Left Brain
(Principles/Rational)

Right Brain
(Pictures/Relational)

LAW

13

IF A PRESENTER SPEAKS OFFENSIVELY, PEOPLE RESPOND DEFENSIVELY

This man persuades men to worship God. (Acts 18:13)

It was said of Dawson Trotman, the founder of The Navigators organization, *in Time* magazine, "He died the way he lived: Always holding someone else up" (*Time,*, July 2, 1956). The fact that he died while rescuing a drowning child from a lake illustrates a vital principle: *People do not care how much you know until they know how much you care.*

During my doctoral classes, I was fortunate to study under Dr. Charles Swindoll. I will never forget his teaching us to make sure that we did not offend the audience, lest we cause them not to listen to our presentation. As a result of Dr. Swindoll's teaching, I began to evaluate each message with the thought, "If a presenter speaks offensively, people will respond defensively." Certain expressions must never be spoken from the pulpit. Ethnic statements, prejudiced comments, "fat jokes," references to physical or mental impairments, or poking fun at the church down the street can crush the very people's spirits that we are called to lift. To communicate to Gutenbergers and Googlers, we must remember that the higher the appreciation, the higher the application.

There can be no doubt that the Apostle Paul cared for the Church and for his fellow servants. As Paul was preparing to graduate for eternity, he showed us how we can finish the ministry course before us. We all know that the goal of ministry is not to strive to please people but rather to please our Lord. Yet, real "men of God" know how to go about delivering the message in a dynamic framework that works *for* them rather than *against* them, that works positively in the long run, rather than negatively in the short run.

In a few words, the Apostle Paul summarized his life. The words about the dying and of the dying are precious to us. Paul's long day work was nearly done. His horizon was darkened by the Church's decaying faith and doctrine. For thirty years, he had traveled a hard road since conversion on the Damascus road.

Paul's life was a failure in the eyes of the world. He suffered the loss of all material things. He was exposed to sorrow, toils, and poverty on missionary journeys. He was hated, despised, laughed at by the Jews and Gentiles, and even forsaken by so-called Christians. The Mamertinum Prison and the beheading axe were the world's wages for him.

Paul had already stood before Nero and knew that martyrdom was near. These familiar verses from 2 Timothy 4:6-8 further paint the portrait of a preacher.

> For I am already being poured out as a drink offering, and the time of my departure has come.
> I have fought the good fight, I have finished the course, I have kept the faith;
> in the future there is laid up for me the crown of righteousness, which the Lord, the righteous Judge, will award to me on that day; and not only to me, but also to all who have loved His appearing.

Paul lays down his arms in Rome and inspires Timothy and the Church to pick them up and carry on the work of Christ. Timothy was to follow in the steps of Paul. Think about it: As Paul's life was coming to a close, he was at the same time moving from addition to multiplication.

In many ways, the Gutenberger has too much Gospel and the Googler does not have enough Gospel. There is a two-way street of communication between these two generations. On this information highway, there is connection or collision. While we build our bridges between these two worlds, if the presenter preaches offensively then the audience will respond defensively. However, this is not to imply that we are trying to win a popularity contest.

Let's back up and get so focused on what God has called us to do, that we will not be misunderstood by the people. The Apostle Paul got really clear with Timothy. He provided the example to pursue our calling as part of the bigger picture. If we do not come to the pulpit with the big picture in mind, if we do not understand what Paul was teaching Timothy, if we do not connect for the people why we are doing our sermons and series, we will not fulfill our commission in ministry. We will end up saying things of correction, which are needed, but the people won't even understand why we are giving correction. They won't understand where we are taking them. People don't mind correction if they understand it is going to get them where they need to go. People need to understand why our message fits in our local church and in their lives. If we have not been focused on where we are going, and people are not aware of where we are taking them, then we will offend people and won't even know it.

We need governing points to help us from being offensive. Paul provides several God-given goals for our ministry. Let's have the discipline to be clear with our people. Paul tells Timothy that if he really pays attention, and is faithful and true to the Scripture, that Timothy can go even farther than Paul did. When we get really focused on this bigger picture, then we will know not only why we started in ministry but also why we stay in the ministry.

MINISTERS SHOULD PURSUE THE COMPLETION OF THEIR COMMISSION BEFORE THE CLOSE OF MINISTRY (v .6)

When we stand before our audience, they must know that we have come to serve them. We are to communicate in a manner of statesmanship, leadership and ownership. When the presenter takes ownership of his or her calling, then he or she will strive to present their best self before others.

At least three distinct ways help to complete our commission. First, we are to complete our commission through *personal service.* There is a definite connection between the personal assertions which the Apostle

Paul is about to make and the solemn charge just given to Timothy. "For I…" contrasts with "but you…" of verse five. Timothy was to fulfill his ministry (v. 5d) because Paul was passing off the scene of history. The work of Christ would have to be done without Paul.

Every Christian is required to serve the Lord *personally.* The minister is to equip the saints, but the believer must perform the principles learned from the sermon. The preacher is to be the personification of the truths applied to the congregation. Each Christian must not depend on the pastor, his staff, or visiting minister to complete the work of Christ. Christianity is lived in the community, not just learned in church.

Second, we complete our commission *through personal sacrifice* (v. 6a). Paul writes figuratively about the close of his ministry with the words, "I am already being poured out as a drink offering . . ." The same verb for "poured out" is used with "sacrifice" in Philippians. This term is used progressively in the present tense to indicate the certainty of the event. The process had begun for Paul.

You may wish to make a study of the Old Testament drink offering (Ex 29:40; Lev 23:13; Num 15:5-10; 28:7). In Numbers 15:1-10, the children of Israel were wandering in the wilderness under the judgment of God. A generation would die because of unbelief and murmuring against God. A new generation would grow up and enter Canaan.

God set the hearts of the new generation on possessing Canaan by giving them sacrificial laws to be followed once they were in the new land. Each Israelite was to offer an unblemished lamb as a sacrifice. None was to be taken by the priest. It symbolized total dedication to God. Each Israelite was to give a meal offering. The drink offering was poured over the sacrificial lamb and meal offering. The larger the animal, the bigger the meal and drink offerings were to be. The drink offering was the final act of sacrifice.

Paul uses symbolic language to express that he had already given himself as a living sacrifice and the meal offering somewhere along life's journey. He had now begun his last act of giving to God. Paul visualized his entire ministry as a offering to God (Rom 15:15-16). He possibly saw himself as the burnt offering, his ministry as the meal offering, and his death as the drink offering. His blood would become a libation offered to God.

We are to be a living sacrifice to fulfill God's will for our lives (Rom 12:1-2). We spend *ourselves* through the preaching of the gospel. Personal sacrifice is required to be effective for Christ. We display emotional sacrifice when friends or family forsake a belief because of our love for God. Sometimes, we may miss a promotion because of righteous standards, or we go to a smaller church rather than a larger to fulfill God's will. At times we have to make a physical sacrifice when we risk our health in order to spread the gospel to unreached peoples.

Ministers are to pour out their lives into the work of Christ and into the lives of people to complete their commission before the close of their ministry. When we study the ministries and messages of spiritual giants, we discover the sacrifices they have paid in order to master themselves privately and master their presentations before others.

When our listeners know we practice what we preach and not just preach what they should practice, our level of leadership rises in the horizons of their minds. We need to find creative ways to let them know that we understand what they may be going through. This does not require a lot of words each week. With the use of technology, we can incorporate a video clip or some pictures without saying anything.

Third, we are to complete our commission through *personal satisfaction* (v. 6b). Personal satisfaction is the result of a completed commission before the end of a ministry. Paul knew he would be beheaded because he was Roman citizen. When the time came, no one stood with him before Nero (2 Tim 4:16-17). Paul knew he had some time left because he asked Timothy to bring the books and parchments, and to come before winter (2 Tim 4:13, 21).

While Paul was in prison, he was productive. He *studied* God's Word—parchments and books. He *spread* the gospel—Crescens to Galatia, Titus to Dalmatia, Tychicus to Ephesus. He *secured* personal relationships (2 Tim 4:11).

Paul viewed death as a "departure." "Departure" can mean "to take down a tent." Paul was a tentmaker. He takes down his tent for the final time to embark on the greatest journey ever. Paul headed toward the house of God. Also, "departure" can mean "to hoist another and set sail." Paul viewed death as release from the world and an opportunity to "set sail" to heaven's peaceful harbor. The storms of life were almost over for Paul.

Most people do not wish to speak about death. They will change the subject like the channels on a television. For the Christian, death is a valley which leads from an earthly pasture to a heavenly home. One can stand before the door of death when one knows that he or she has done one's best for the Lord.

Yet, we must keep in mind that it is possible to expend all our energies and talents for God without worrying about the future. Christ has taken the doom out of death and the gloom out of the grave. The minister can approach his pastoral and evangelistic duties with the perspective that the worst thing has already been taken care of by Christ, and the best things are yet ahead. Since we know that our future is secured, we press forward with the preaching of the Gospel with all our might.

When we stand to share the faith, we also must show our feelings. The early Church knew that Paul loved them due to the stark reality of what he endured for them. He not only articulated the heart of God, but showed his sacrifice before the Church. There were numerous instances that Paul had to speak bluntly to local churches but they knew that they knew he spoke to them out of love.

MINISTERS SHOULD PURSUE
THE COMPLETION OF THEIR COMMISSION DURING
THE COURSE OF MINISTRY (v. 7)

We have at least three ways to achieve this second goal.

Spiritual Discernment

We can complete the course of our ministry through *spiritual discernment* (v. 7a). In verse six, Paul wrote in the present tense about how to die. In verse seven, he instructs in the perfect tense how to live. His past accomplishments carry into the present. Paul left the earth with no regrets because his task was finished. Literally, verse seven reads: "I have finished, the faith I have kept."

"I have fought the good fight..." could be translated, "I have agonized the agony." The picture is most likely not a warfare, but as we have said previously would most aptly express excessive effort and expended energy against a powerful opponent in some kind of athletic contest (1 Co 9:25; 1 Tim 6:12).

Christians, and especially preachers, need to realize they are involved in a spiritual struggle. We must possess a drive to succeed over the enemy. We battle against inconsistencies and distractions which cause one to settle for the good things, which become bad things when they stop us from receiving the best things. We are to wrestle against materialism. We are to fight to keep our relationship with Christ updated. Maximum energy is required to win in the spiritual life. To complete our life victoriously, constant vigilance is required every day. Trivial pursuits do not produce triumph at life's end. The preaching of the gospel is the most noble cause in the universe.

As we study and prepare our presentations for particular audiences, we should ask the Lord for spiritual discernment and expect to receive it. When I talk to the local leaders where I speak, I ask what subjects have been preached in recent weeks. It is my goal to discern what the congregation needs and to be in sync with the local church. Wrong discernment equals wrong direction. Be sure not to ask your audience to do something that you have not already done. They will see right through you!

Spiritual Discipline

Second, we can complete the course of our ministry through *spiritual discipline* (v. 7b). "I have finished the course" displays completed action with continuing results. "Course" means "foot race." "Finished" simply means "to complete or arrive at the goal." Paul stressed that in his life as a Christian, he had accomplished the ministry to which the Lord had called him. The Apostle's eyes, like those of a runner's, were riveted at all times on the finishing post. This has been a scheduled race which he had to run. To the Ephesian elders he said, "But I do not consider my life of any account as dear to myself, so that I may finish my course and the ministry which I received from the Lord Jesus, to testify solemnly of the gospel of the grace of God" (Acts 20:24).

Ministers get off course several ways. Excessive baggage can cause one to stumble in the race. Take off any weight that holds you back from reaching the finish line of a completed ministry (Heb. 12:1). A clear-cut focus helps keep us on course. Studying God's Word, seeking

God's face in prayer, and sharing the gospel on a personal basis will keep us on course.

Besetting sin will thrust us off course. We must fix our eyes on Jesus. Run the race with patience. Realize that this race is a marathon, not just a one hundred meter dash. We are not competing with other Christians to the finish line. The object is to finish our God-given ministry before the end of our life.

Wasting time will keep our race from being finished. Ours is a scheduled race. All preachers are running against the clock. All the time spent off course is a loss to the race. Life's end could come before the race is finished. We should not be slaves to time, but should redeem it. As my friend James Merritt has aptly stated, the big question is not whether we will finish our race but whether we will win it. A race half done is a race undone.

Maybe we should stop and think about the finish if we are ever going to focus. We could probably all think of a ministers who have hobbies or sports yet has failed to improve themselves or their ministry and still preaches the same way even though the world around them changed. For example, tell me what is the official color of a "yield" sign? If you answer "yellow," then you do not realize that yield signs have not been yellow in nearly twenty years! Yield signs are now red and white. As we run this race in ministry, we are to exercise our spiritual muscles and make the necessary changes to reach maximum effectiveness when we preach the Word before people.

Spiritual Dedication

When we preach the Word of God, some people become mad while others become glad. Our task is not same as one who gives a lecture on leadership or a message on management. Our God-called assignment is to communicate the Gospel in a manner that our listeners can understand and apply to their lives. However, if people do become offended, it should not be due to our lack of sensitivity or sensibility.

We can complete our course in ministry through *spiritual dedication* (v. 7c). "Kept" means "remain faithful or true." "Faith" is an allusion to the pledge that athletes made to obey the rules in the public games. Paul had been faithful to the rules in fighting the good fight and finishing the race. He had been faithful to his commitment to Christ.

In the final analysis, the Christian life is a personal matter. The minister must first apply God's Word to his life before he effectively applies it to his audience. The struggle against spiritual wickedness and the race to complete our ministry are designed to build strong Christian character. If we are unfairly pushed out of the boxing ring, we must keep our faith in God. This world is not to be our garden of sinful delights. Spiritual dedication is the place where the Christian wins the grand fight, finishes the race and keeps the commitment to Christ.

MINISTERS SHOULD PURSUE THE COMPLETION OF THEIR COMMISSION FOR THE CROWN OF MINISTRY (v. 8)

A huge spirit does not become offended with a small irritation. If someone or something has offended us, we cannot take that offense to the pulpit. If we do, it will come out in our presentation with a tone that is not loving or gracious, but condescending and offensive. We are to challenge our listeners to lift their spiritual eyes higher and not be entangled with small things either.

We are able to finish our ministry because of *its preservation* (v. 8a). Paul was the wrestler who won the match, the boxer who fought a good fight and the runner who finished the course to win the race. He kept his eyes on the eternal reward. He desired to motivate Timothy by telling him why preaching the Word was *worth it.*

The Greek term for "there is laid up" is in the present tense because Paul was still adding to this reward. His reward was safely stored away. No enemy would be able to deprive Paul of his eternal reward. The words for this reward were used in association with outstanding athletes receiving their public reward.

"The crown of righteousness" will be given to Paul because he fought successfully, ran satisfactorily and kept the faith steadfastly. The "crown" is the victor's crown. The Roman athlete who won was awarded a laurel wreath or garland of oak leaves on his head. Literally, Paul wrote, "a crown which is righteousness." It is not the crown which will bring final justification, but it refers to the permanent and perfect state of righteousness. The Christian will experience the absence of sin forever and enjoy the presence of God.

The preacher will not be primarily rewarded for his strength or skill, but for his service. The crown is based on the character displayed during the fight and the race.

We are able to finish our ministry because of *its provider* (v. 8b-c). The "Lord" who will give the crown of righteousness is Christ, since Paul identifies Him with "the righteous judge." Jesus is both righteous and supreme judge. There are possibly two implied contrasts in this passage. First, an unrighteous Nero handed down a wrong judgment against Paul. Second, the Olympic judges were not always impartial in their decisions. Christ is always correct in His decisions and would set the record straight on "that day" (2 Tim. 1:12, 18).

The minister and his congregation are commissioned to proclaim God's Word and let the Lord make earthly injustice correct when He returns. We are not to take matters into our own hands because of biases and inconsistencies. Christians who maintain righteousness now will have eternal righteousness given to them "on that day." Life is not always fair, but God is always just.

Are we striving to fulfill the God-given for our life and ministry? Can we with complete integrity get on our knees and ask God to provide for us? Do we believe enough in our ministry to stand alone if necessary in order to please the Lord? When we accomplish what we are working on, what will we have? Is our life and ministry bringing glory to God in every aspect? Can we truthfully ask the Lord to be our provider in the time of trouble?

We are able to finish our ministry because of *its prospect* (v. 8d). Paul included every Christian when he wrote, "but also to all who have loved his appearing." The perfect tense of "have loved" suggests they have loved His appearing in the pastor and will continue to do so in the future even till the receiving of the reward. Any Christian who truly yearns for Christ's coming will be eligible for the "crown of righteousness."

Every preacher in general and Christian in specificity should strive to accomplish as much as possible before Christ returns. The basis of Paul's admonition is the return of Christ (2 Tim. 4:1). Our soul-winning should be intended to win the unsaved before Jesus comes back. The preacher should proclaim his sermon as though it is the last one preached before the coming of Christ. Our missionary giving ought to reflect our belief in the coming of Christ.

Dr. Mark Buntain or, as some call him "St. Mark of Calcutta," and his wife, Huldah, arrived in Calcutta in October 1954, expecting to serve as missionaries to India for about a year. God turned that one year into a fruitful ministry in India that still thrives today. Dr. Buntain was born and raised in Canada. When he was called to Calcutta, he did not want to go. But he denied himself and followed God's call on his life.

When they arrived in Calcutta, their ministry started out in a tent, which later grew into an enormous ministry center. They built a school to educate the people about God's love and to raise up Christian leaders. But Mark noticed that many of his students were too weak to study, so he started a feeding program. While he led a life of sacrifice, he fed hundreds and eventually thousands of children each day. The school turned into a one-bed hospital, which later became a hospital called the "Mission of Mercy." Their motto over the door read "Jesus Heals." This 120-bed hospital gave medical care to many people, including their friend Mother Teresa.

There are greater compassion ministries in the world today, but with this one, on two different occasions I was privileged to hear Mark Buntain preach the Word of God. Even after twenty years, his words ring in my ears. He said in both presentations, "If I had one thousand lives, I would give them all to Calcutta."

There was no doubt that Buntain loved India and wanted that nation to come to Christ. We also stand on the boundary of two worlds. We forsake this world's comforts and store up treasures of heaven. The minister endures the injustice of the present world so he can enjoy the justice of the one to come.

Suppose you were invited into an open field to view an I-beam before it was hoisted to hold together the large roof of a major new superstructure. Upon arriving, you are invited to walk the length of it, 129 feet and 12 inches wide. A man offers you $100 if you can do it, and you smile as you walk because it is the easiest $100 you ever earned. Next, construction cranes lift the I-beam ten feet in the air, and the man asks if you'll walk across it for $1,000. Once again, you smile because it seems to be an easy $1,000.

But then, the man shows you a picture of the Petronas Twin Towers in Kuala Lumpur, Malaysia, soaring more than 1,400 feet high and standing 129 feet apart. He offers you $10,000 if you will walk across the top of the same kind of I-beam that you have already walked across. This time, you refuse. "No!" you tell him, "There is no way that I would walk across that chasm for $10,000 or even $100,000!"

After showing you that picture, the man shows you a gritty picture of your child being held hostage on one end of the I-beam, up at the 1400-foot mark. He says, "You will either walk across that I-beam from one tower to the next, or you will witness your child being thrown from the top of the building."

What would you do now? Would you reconsider walking across from one side to the other? Would you take the risk in order to save your child? It is amazing how quickly life changes when we come face to face with what really matters most.

When we stand in front of our listeners, we need to come to grips with the understanding that everyone before us has human needs. Many of them are facing serious crises. We cross the chasm to reach them, then bring them back across to safety. It is our responsibility to compel them to walk across the I-beam, from one side of their understanding about a subject to the other side. In other words, they need to be compelled to move from indecision to a decision because of hearing our presentation.

Christ loved us so much that crossed the ultimate I-beam from heaven to earth so that we could be redeemed from utter catastrophe for eternity. Christ took that "love walk" to the cross so humankind can be free from the tyranny of Satan who wants to hold this world hostage forever. When we cross the I-beam of our listeners' understanding, we will witness more positive responses to the Gospel than ever before.

We serve as the bridge between a sinful world and a sacred God. It is imperative for us to see ourselves the way God sees us so we will preach with tears, reaching out to a lost world. But we are careful with the pulpit, because when we preach offensively, people will respond defensively.

Left Brain
(Principles/Rational)

Right Brain
(Pictures/Relational)

Law 1:	Fill the Pulpit	Law 2:	Buy on Emotion
Law 3:	Begin with the End in Mind	Law 4:	Giving Birth to Barbwire
Law 5:	Turn Ears to Eyes	Law 6:	Pray Yourself to Life
Law 7:	The Great Sword of Truth	Law 8:	Mind Craves Order
Law 9:	The Private Discipline	Law 10:	The Picture Gallery
Law 11:	The Clock and the Crowd	Law 12:	Knowing the Audience
Law 13:	Offensively Equals Defensively	**Law 14:**	**Timing Is Everything**
Law 15:	From Reasons to Visions	Law 16:	Becoming Unpredictable
Law 17:	Polished Transitions	Law 18:	Humor to Heart
Law 19:	The First Ninety Seconds	Law 20:	Give More than Expected

LAW

14

THE DIFFERENCE BETWEEN A FOUL BALL AND A HOME RUN IS TIMING

Preach the word; be ready in season and out of season. (2 Tim 4:2)

y wife and I enjoy Hawaii. We just do. We went for our honeymoon and have gone almost every year since, to celebrate our anniversary, take a vacation, or enjoy our family Christmas. Each time, we plan for months, save our money, reserve our favorite spot, buy our airline tickets to get the best seats, prepare our house to be vacated, and plan our clothes to be packed.

Most ministers likely do the same with their favorite destination or pastime. And yet, if I were to ask about the message they will be unpacking in six months, nine out of ten will not be able to pinpoint it. There may be vague advance thought but little price paid in study, even less in reserving the time with the various church departments to ensure they are ready to help illustrate the message. There is scarce thought to the messages that will lead up to it, the words used to clothe the idea, or the follow-up plan for the resulting change that comes to the congregation as a result of the message. *We all know how to do better, so let's do it!*

Great baseball players learn fast that there is a difference between a foul ball and a home run. To hit the ball over the fence, the timing has to be impeccable. People do not come to church to watch us hit foul balls each week. We may limp out of a presentation thinking, "If only

I'd had more time," when the truth is, we just didn't see the fast ball coming. If we cannot see and judge the kind of ball, we will swing too late and have the foul balls to show for it.

Timing is the key to hitting straight a golf ball, kicking a soccer ball through the goal, or smacking a tennis ball across the net to win a championship. Timing is everything. People today will not come to a presentation to hear someone teach a subject completely wrong. Several areas of timing need our attention in order to help advance our listeners around the bases, down the field or into the victory circle.

A PRESENTATION SERIES NEEDS TO BE TIMED CORRECTLY

For an athlete to hit a ball, the eyes have to remain on the ball. Without a correct understanding of where the ball is or where the athlete is in the big picture of the game, he or she will not have the right sense of timing.

When presenters have a skewed world view, their message could be out of sync, yet they wouldn't know it. I learned a long time ago that in any sizable audience there are people with a basic knowledge about many different subjects. If I present a message with outdated information, invariably someone will come up to me to share some updated information. Having outdated information means we are out of touch with the times. Overall, Gutenbergers are more patient than Googlers. Googlers will sit online and fact-check your message while you are giving it. If a Googler senses that you are not qualified to present the message, then he or she will quickly tune you out as "irrelevant to where I live my life."

Whether you are a pastor who brings one or more than one presentation each week or a professional public speaker, it is important to plan months ahead in your research, thought processes, filing and goal setting. Half of the battle is deciding what you will speak on and then having the time to fill in the presentation. When the batter is at the plate or the tennis player is at the service line or the soccer player draws near the goal, half the battle is knowing when to swing.

Many presenters wait to the last moment to decide what to say and how to say it. When a presentation does not come across as organized or the thought processes are shallow, then people know this person did not sow early enough to have a powerful presentation. The result is not just a foul ball but at times an opportunity lost forever.

When the pastor is planning a series, thought needs to be given as to what will be preached before and after the series. The point is to think "big picture" in the world and "local picture" in the community. Where do we wish the congregation to be regarding the topic when we are completed with the series? What are the top five outcomes? Will it require one or more series to achieve these outcomes? Do we want to have a few guest speakers to flesh out this subject or theme for the audience? Do we need to involve the choir, the drama team, the video department, or even the children's ministries? The better we know the subject or theme, the greater flexibility we have when we need to make changes. For example, if there is a national or international event that needs to be addressed, then the series needs to be interrupted to demonstrate timeliness.

EVERY PRESENTATION SHOULD NOT BE PERFORMED THE SAME WAY

The story is told of two laymen having breakfast, talking about their pastors. One said, "Our pastor's message always sounds like, 'Ding, Dong. Ding, Dong.'" The other said, "Well, at least you have some variety. We only hear, 'Ding, Ding, Ding, Ding.'"

Every athlete has a unique style. Even though the game is the same, it is played differently, without breaking the rules. Some batters get close to the plate. Some soccer players lean forward. Some tennis players use both hands for their backhands. Although the outcome hoped for is the same, athletes go about it in different ways.

There are countless ways a presentation can be delivered. Use technology. However, when the audience is more intrigued with your gadgets than your message, then you know that you have gone too far. If it takes sensation to get a crowd, it will take sensation to keep a crowd, and eventually you will run out of enough sensation to keep the crowd interested. We have to use balance without becoming boring.

I previously advocated moving the presentation to different times during a reoccurring event, like church services, business meetings, or annual conference. There are at least two reasons for this variety. First, when we move the time of the presentation, the level of our communication increases due to becoming less predictable. Second, different strategies or desired outcomes sometime require the presentation to be placed in a different timeframe. If, for example, you want a lengthy prayer meeting after your presentation in the church service, then placing the presentation up front allows time for this outcome. Sometimes, we may be more effective to share half of the presentation at the beginning of the worship service and the second half at the end. The point is to use a sense of timing for our advantage in order to hold our audience's attention.

You are in control of your presentation. Your timing is the difference between a foul ball and a home run!

THE STUDY TIME OF THE PRESENTER NEEDS TO BE DEVELOPED FOR MAXIMUM EFFECTIVENESS

If a chef does not make a routine of shopping for fresh ingredients and doing "prep work" before the meal is called for, then no matter how great the chef, the meal will suffer. A successful routine reduces the amount of preparation time required and increases the level of weekly results. The presenter who is always accessible to people will not hit many home runs.

I have been privileged to see the private offices of some of the greatest ministers of the last century and today. From how their office is arranged and the books being read, I can gain a pretty good idea of how that pastor preaches without even hearing one message. Here are some effective steps I have learned which you may consider while developing your study time for your speaking time.

1. Strategize your speaking calendar one year in advance.

Open a blank calendar and look through the entire year, making specific decisions relating to big family days, vacation time and all of the red letter days on the church calendar. Make decisions first and foremost that allow you to get the big rocks in, the most important themes and subjects, before anything crowds them out. Keep in mind that some years there are fifty-three Sundays. Think carefully when you want to have guest speakers and when you would like to have your pastoral team preach on certain weekends.

2. Systematize your speaking opportunities one year in advance.

Once we have carefully strategized our calendar, then we need to systematize the number of times we will speak. Until this step is done, we are not able to decide how many hours we need to devote to study time before speaking time. What is the difference between strategizing a year in advance and systematizing your calendar a year in advance? When you are strategizing, you are thinking about where you are going and where you want your congregation to be one year in advance. When systematizing, you are creating reproducible methods that will help you to achieve the strategic goals you have for your congregation. Effective methods increase success.

3. Select the subjects to be presented on specific dates.

This is where decision-making becomes more complex and concrete. It is one thing to observe the big picture, strategize your thinking, and systematize your opportunities. It is a different level now to decide your series and themes for the entire year. Every decision has a destiny, and every choice has a chain. Think about Bible books or verses you wish to preach and teach in the next year. Evaluate the different themes you have preached on in previous years and determine which ones you should consider teaching in the next twelve months.

After you have decided how many times you are going to speak in the next twelve months and the subjects and themes, it is now time to put your study time on the calendar. Allocate the time it takes you to prepare, multiplied by the number of presentations in your weekly calendar. This is where we learn to hit singles, doubles, triples, and then home runs, rather than striking out or hitting a foul ball. This is the timeframe when champions are developed for success in life and ministry.

A wise presenter lets his or her team know the presenter's schedule, so they can add value to the presentations as well. Some ministers have a drama team working on an illustrated sermon three months in advance. Some have more than one worship team to minister message-specific songs or even dress in particular clothing to enhance the message.

Others assign a soloist or choir number to be well-rehearsed in advance. Having people working on your message, besides you, creates a sense of expectancy in the entire congregation and helps to increase success.

The mind is an amazing machine. Once the mind has been given a specific goal, it will continue to dwell on this information until the goal is completed.

4. Study Your Presentation Beginning with the End in Mind

Once you have determined the purpose of the presentation, or the outcomes you desire to have, immediately think through the invitation. This kind of advanced thinking brings the kind of creativity and variety we seek for the long term. In other words, we don't want the same kind of response for every presentation. Advanced thinking forces us to live our lives in shoe leather where our listeners are every day of their lives. As we prepare our message, we should imaginatively invite different kinds of people to our desk and ask, "How does this message apply to him or her?

Ministers need to think ahead on every level, from strategy to study, so our communication level continues to grow ever higher. When we use a "two hours ahead of the hounds" philosophy, almost everything is left to the last moments or days instead of weeks or months. Great presentations require great thinking ahead of time. We will never be able to speak from the overflow of our lives unless we spend quality time investing into our souls.

Statistically, athletes who think through and know who and what they are up against, as well as the potential obstacles, increase their potential for success by more than ninety percent. Batters study pitchers and pitchers study the different batters. Soccer players watch videos of other teams. Tennis players know their opponents, and golfers study golf courses. If we want to score some points every time we step up to bring a presentation, we will invest quality time sizing up people, potential and problems.

Throughout the year, we can keep our eye on the ball by staying focused on the calendar, knowing the dates that are coming and the presentations that will need to be made. We size up the opponent by looking for and expecting unforeseen obstacles that will no doubt come our way. If we prepare ahead of time, we will score more points consistently during our presentations. Part of the timing element is learning your own average amount of time needed to prepare a message. We have to learn to pace ourselves on a weekly basis so we can effectively run for years to come.

The late Dr. Adrian Rogers prepared more than 6,000 different sermons, with an average length of ten to twelve double-spaced pages. He had a specific study routine and strategic process for development and delivery that allowed him to produce this enormous amount of dynamic content, week after week, for fifty years. During his preaching career, his office at church was used for meetings, but he kept his personal study private. During those years, he had fewer than 10 people, outside of family, enter his study. What we value the most, we protect its sanctity. I was fortunate to go inside his private study on December 15, 2008.

"Joyce, how did Adrian prepare his weekly messages?" I asked his wife. She walked me around through his study and shared with me Dr. Rogers' process of success.

Dr. Rogers had three desks in his study, and he regularly preached three times per week. He used one desk for Sunday morning messages, another desk for Sunday evening, and a third desk, the largest one, for Wednesday evening and sermon series. On each of these desks were the files and books pertaining to those messages he was working on at that time. Though your method may vary, the point I wish to make here is that Dr. Rogers had a pattern, a path, and a process he developed that served him well for many, many years and helped him to become arguably one of the most prolific sermonizers of the last century.

The difference in a win or loss in any game is timing. If the timing is off, the ball will not get into play. When our timing is consistently "on" relating to our calendar, culture, and communication, we will find that most of our messages are exceptional instead of finding ourselves settling for average.

We attract what we *are*, not what we *want*. As we grow as a presenter and our messages mature, the audience will come to our presentations with a high appreciation of our thinking capacity and speaking ability. If our professional lives outpace our personal lives, then stress will be the result to us personally and to those around us. Throughout the years, our personal development must outpace our ministerial lives. Otherwise, we will fail due to not taking the time every week to grow more. Sure, we need to know the time, but in most cases it is our own timing that makes the difference.

I have been honored to serve on the Board of Directors for Evangelism Explosion International along with some great leaders such as Richard DeVos, the founder of the Amway Corporation. In one of our meetings, I asked for his thoughts on the economic crisis the nation was undergoing. He said, "When we began Amway fifty years ago, it was in a most difficult economic climate. *We may not like the season we are in, but it is the only season we have.* We cannot choose the season, but we can choose how we will use the season we have."

He went on to say, "As Christians, we are called to do all we can, with the resources we have to finish the Great Commission." When we know our times and can enact excellent timing, we will hit more home runs and less foul balls!

Left Brain
(Principles/Rational)

Right Brain
(Pictures/Relational)

LAW

15

PEOPLE DO NOT JUST WANT TO HEAR REASONS BUT TO SEE VISIONS

Sir, we wish to see Jesus. (Jn 12:21)

In my family, going back at least three generations, all the boys have been named "James." I have an uncle "Jay," my dad is "Jim," and I also have an identical twin brother. Yes, my parents never struggled to call us by the right name because even though we look and sound identical, we also share the identical name, James. For many years now, my brother has done a remarkable job as Vice President of Development at Southeastern University, Lakeland, Florida. A lot of pranks and laughter filled the years to lead us to where we each are today as ministers in fulltime Christian service.

One of the highlights of our teen years was going each summer to a Christian camp in Alabama. On one occasion, during the morning chapel service, my brother slumped his head down almost into his lap and fell into an exhausted sleep. He slept through the rest of the message. When the audience was asked to stand, he remained sound asleep. When the invitation began, and the young people began to move forward for a time of prayer around the front of the auditorium, he was still out of it, crumpled into his own lap. When the service concluded, the entire camp went to the lunchroom, nearly a third of a mile away. But he remained unaffected and sound asleep! After lunch, my friends and I took the camp director back to the chapel and after shaking him out of that sleep, he finally realized he had slept through the sermon, the altar response, and lunch. We still howl with laughter about it!

How many times do we think we are connecting and communicating to our audience when in fact they are light years away in their thinking and completely oblivious to our message? We may preach out our very souls, yet they do not even hear us, much less respond. The presenter needs to cultivate the ability to pull the audience close and not let them go until they have made a decision to participate in the call to action.

If we are not careful, we will say more and more about less and less, without solving the big issues of life. We have to remember that most people we speak to are just trying to get through another day. We must choose creative metaphors and build bridges from the ancient biblical past to contemporary realities. How people view the preacher has a lot to do with how they will listen and respond to the message. Our sermon does not begin when we open our mouths to speak, but when we are first seen in the church service. People are constantly sizing us up during the worship time and the giving of the offering.

Bert Decker outlines the nine skills that develop energy, openness, and visual interest, falling into three categories (Decker, 79). These are:

Eye Factor:
    1. Eye communication
    2. Posture and movement
    3. Facial expressions and gestures
    4. Dress and appearance

Energy Factor:
    5. Voice and vocal variety
    6. Language and non-words
    7. Listener involvement
    8. Humor

Example Factor:
    9. Natural Self

These skills are simple to acquire and sharpen.

EYE FACTOR

The visual sense is powerful. The nerve pathways of the eye to the brain are twenty-five times larger than the nerve pathways from the ear to the brain. The eye is the only sensory organ that contains brain cells. Memory improvement experts invariably emphasize techniques that link the information you want to remember to visual images. A huge body of research has been amassed, demonstrating that of all the sensory input the brain registers, the visual input makes the greatest impact. It is the visual sense which dominates all of the senses.

Why is the visual sense so dominant? It is estimated that the nerve endings of eyes are struck by literally 700,000 stimuli every instant. We cannot escape the massive impact of this bombardment on our brain. Psychologists have said that viewing something three times has the power of one actual experience. This fact alone has enormous consequence. The power of vision can be used for good or ill. But there is no question that it is a strong power. (Decker, 82)

The advent of television has exaggerated this natural visual dominance. Today's adults were raised on television and are much more visually sophisticated than their parents. Clearly, the visual channel communicates with power and impact. To communicate effectively in today's business and social world, you must be aware of the language of the right brain—and you must use it. The language of the right brain is a visual language. The eye factor dominates our presentations.

The Inconsistent Message

A spoken message is made up of only three components: *the verbal, the vocal, and the visual.* Professor Albert Mehrabian of UCLA conducted a landmark study on the relationships between the presenter and listener regarding three specific components and the believability of our message. The verbal element is the message—the words you say. Most of us tend to concentrate only on the verbal element, mistakenly assuming this to be the message, when in fact it is only part of the message. (Decker, 83)

The second part of the message is the vocal element—the intonation, projection and resonance of your voice as it carries the words. It is the feeling behind the words or expressions. The audience has to feel your emotion behind your words.

The third part is the visual element—what people see—the motion and expression of your body and face as you speak. The more these three factors harmonize with each other, the more believable you are as a speaker. What happens when these three components contradict each other? We transmit an inconsistent message. We literally send mixed signals. For example, when you appear nervous, awkward or under pressure, your verbal content is blocked by your inconsistent vocal and visual message. Your words will not be trusted because it is the visual channel that dominates what is believed. Which signals will our listener find the most convincing? Which signal will our listener believe and which signal will be ignored? The visual is believed more than vocal and verbal. (Decker, 83)

When we learn how to coordinate all three of these components to form one totally consistent message, we are not only believable, we have persuasive power. The excitement and enthusiasm of your voice work with the energy and animation of your face and body to reflect the conviction of your message. When your words, your voice, and your delivery all work in harmony, your message dramatically and persuasively saturates your listener's mind.

Visual Aids

Visuals trump vocabulary. When visuals were used in teaching a course on vocabulary, learning improved 200 percent. (Decker, 85) What does the visual channel tell the listener about us when we send out an inconsistent message? Perhaps it says we are insincere or lacking in confidence. Or perhaps we have something to hide. Remember the old axiom, "What you see is what you get." This statement applies to personal impact.

Eye communication: The number one skill to be aware of and work on is eye communication. Ralph Waldo Emerson said, "An eye can threaten like a loaded and leveled gun; or can insult like hissing and kicking or in its altered mood by means of kindness, make the heart dance with joy." (Decker, 85). Eye communication is your number one skill. Eye communication does not just mean good eye contact, but learn to communicate to your listeners by what you choose them to see during your presentation. It ranks first because it has the greatest impact in both one-on-one communications and large group communications. It literally connects mind to mind, since your eyes are the only part of your central nervous system that are in direct contact with another human being. When your eyes meet the eyes of another person, you make a connection. When you fail to make that connection, it matters very little what you say.

Involvement through eye contact: Use involvement rather than intimacy or intimidation. Intimacy and intimidation mean looking at another person steadily for a long period—say, ten seconds to a minute or more. In business and normal social conversations, both intimacy or intimidation make our listeners feel uncomfortable. Over 90 percent of our business and social communications calls for involvement. (Decker, 88)

For effective eye communication, when you look at someone count to five. A feeling of involvement requires about five seconds of steady eye contact. This is the average amount of time we need to complete a thought or a sentence. This is usually the normal amount of time to build confidence without stepping over the line and making a person feel smothered.

Posture

"Dress for success" is an old axiom. But the most powerful visual first impression you make comes not from your clothes but from your posture. How you hold yourself physically is an indicator of how you hold yourself mentally—and a decisive factor in how others regard you. Do you lean on one leg? Do you slouch? Do you move around?

Here are some basic rules to remember:

Stand tall. Poor upper body posture often reflects low self-esteem. Stand with your shoulders back and your stomach in. Whether you are walking into a room or speaking before an audience, for maximum visual impact stand straight and move naturally.

Watch your lower body. The second part of posture that often gets neglected is the lower body. When speaking to others, you may limit your effectiveness and squander your communication energy through inappropriate body language. Do you rock back and forth? Do you pace? Does your posture speak positively about you? The most common posture problem is leaning back on one hip. This position communicates, "I don't want to be here," and literally distances you from your listener. Remember the goal is to close the gap between us and our listeners. (Decker, 91-95)

Get in the Ready Position. The Ready Position means "weight forward." Communication rides on energy. Your posture either communicates energy and interest to your listener's mind—or it communicates apathy and disinterest. When you are speaking confidently from a self-assured stance, your energy is directed forward, physically and psychologically, toward your listener. The Ready Position looks like this: Lean slightly forward, knees somewhat flexed, so you can bounce lightly on the balls on your feet. You should feel like an athlete ready to move easily and quickly in any direction.

Move. Tradition says speakers should always be rooted to one spot when they speak. Tradition is wrong! To make emotional contact with our listeners, we need to convey excitement, enthusiasm, and confidence when we speak. That means we have to move. Motion is visual. Motion is energetic. Be fluid instead of being stiff while speaking. We will be more apt to move people to action if we actually move during our presentation.

Dress and Appearance

John Molloy wrote in the 1970s some timeless wisdom: "You never get a second chance to make a good first impression."

After posture, the most immediate visual impression we make on our listener's first impressions are made up of our dress and appearance. The two by four rule: The impressions made in the first two seconds are so vivid that it takes another four minutes to add fifty percent more impression—negative or positive—to that communication. And those first two seconds are almost entirely visual, made up how we look before them. This means that if we make a poor first impression, even before we open our mouth, it takes a long time to overcome the damage done. (Decker, 98, 100)

Since 90 percent of your body is covered with clothing, the way you dress is crucially important. Yet, the 10 percent of your body which is not covered by clothes is the most crucial—your face and hair. When you are speaking, your listener's eyes are largely influenced by the way groom yourself from the neck up—hairstyle, make up, and jewelry if you are a woman. Hairstyle and facial hair, or lack of it, if you are a man.

Be Appropriate. There is not so much a right or wrong way to dress as there is an appropriate way. This means you should first be appropriate to your environment and, second, be appropriate to yourself. You should dress and groom to make others comfortable with you.

Gestures and Smile

Are you aware of how you look to others? Do you smile? Do you have awkward or annoying gestures? Do you have a nervous gesture? Do you smile?

Your listener's mind is wary and watchful. It is looking for the nonverbal cues that prove you can be believed and trusted. People know that if we believe what we are saying, we will be animated while we are saying it.

Few things are more effective than open gestures and a warm, open smile. An open-armed greeting is welcoming. It says, "Come in." I often spread my arms as I gesture, as if about to embrace the whole audience. Your smile dominates your listener's impression of you as you communicate. A smile shows not only on your mouth but in and around your eyes. It demonstrates openness and likability.

Gestures and smiles are the dominant visual component of spoken communication. Our gestures and smiles reveal our inner state and propel our message with energy and emotional force. Your goal is to become a natural communicator. Keep your hands and arms relaxed at your sides when you are at rest. When your message calls for animation, enthusiasm, and underscoring, gesture naturally. (Decker, 105)

ENERGY FACTOR

There is nothing mystical to unlocking inner energy. We have to learn to pack more energy into our presentations for powerful impact.

Voice And Vocal Variety

Your voice is the vehicle of your message. Learn to drive that vehicle like a fine car, a Lamborghini. Push it, open it up! The voice is an expressive instrument. Our listener's mind is finely attuned to the signals carried in the voice. A single word you speak can reveal volumes of information about you. Your voice is what gets you where you need to go. Your voice should convert energy.

Make your voice naturally authoritative. Imagine your voice as a roller coaster, with up and down variety. Be aware of your telephone voice. Put your real feelings into your voice. Do you know how to put a smile into your voice? Once you really hear your voice, you will be able to change your voice.

Record your voice. Your vocal tone and quality can account for up to 84 percent of your message when you are not seen by anyone, for example, when you are on the phone. Use the power of the pause. Pauses add power to your presentation. Pause at important points or phrases.

When we master voice and vocal variety, we are more effective on the telephone. We convey emotions when we have a flexible voice. Our voice can be made attractive to the ear; capable of emphasizing certain points and ideas with energy (Decker, 125-33).

Words and Non-Words

Another good way to put the Energy Factor in our communication is through our use of words. To put the energy of lightning in our message, we have to select the right words for the right situations. We should develop a good, rounded vocabulary. "A word fitly spoken," we read in Proverbs 25:11, "is like apples of gold in pictures of silver." With just a little bit of effort every day, we can make apples of gold every time we speak. Remember: Our goal is not to impress but to make an impression!

Non-Words

Everyone knows that language is made of words. But did you know that language is also made of non-words? To communicate effectively, we must be aware of non-words that obstruct our message. The most common non-words are "uhh," "ahh," and "umm." The wrong non-words bleed the energy out of our presentations. When the energy level is low, the confidence in the listener regarding the speaker is low.

There are several steps to overcoming the negative nonwords and maintaining energy throughout your presentation. First, find your level of nonwords. Listen to yourself on a recording. Count the nonwords you use. Second, replace your nonwords with something more powerful.

Third, use the power of the pause. You can pause for as long as three or four seconds, right in the middle of a sentence—and it will not have a negative impact on your listeners. (Decker, 130-35)

THE EXAMPLE FACTOR

You have no doubt learned throughout this book the importance of being yourself. God created you and made no one else in the world like you. Only you can create certain elements that represent who you are in the world. We should strive to learn from others but not become a copycat of others. When we settle only to adopt what others do and how others present, we have chosen to be less than the person the Lord has created us to become.

Over the years, I have literally given more than 7,000 presentations and counting. To do so, I studied what others did and how they presented. But, this study and reflection did not cause me to stop growing as a presenter. Rather, they improved my presentation skills. Some elements that I used to employ I no longer use because I simply found a better way by watching, reading and practicing. Other elements have been foundational stones of my entire ministry career.

When we settle on mimicking other people, our listeners have an intuition that tells them that something is missing in our lives. The result is that our level of trust is lowered and the gap is widened between us and our audience. There is something about listening to speakers who are teaching out of personal life experience. They know what they are talking about. When style and substance connect, there is a powerful presence and persuasion that impacts listeners at the heart level and not just the head level.

Our goal is to connect, motivate, and change our listeners' point of view. When the Eye Factor, Energy Factor, and Example Factor come together, we experience maximum impact in the audience. People leave our presentations saying, "The light came on for me. I saw something in a different way. My mind has been changed. I start making the necessary changes today."

Left Brain
(Principles/Rational)

Right Brain
(Pictures/Relational)

LAW

16

THE LOWEST FORM OF
COMMUNICATION
IS PREDICTABILITY

When the Pharisee saw it, he was surprised. (Lk 11:38)

Since my early teens spent sitting on the front row of church, I have collected not just books for my library but also recorded sermons. Sheri and I moved across country a short time ago in order to increase our ability to be effective in ministry. She tried to persuade me not to bring thousands of audio cassettes piled in boxes and stacked in the closets of my former office. The old audio recordings look to the Google mind like dinosaurs. To me, they are precious, rare treasures, nuggets of gold from preachers of a bygone era that are invaluable to my study, my soul and spirit. I have listened to thousands of hours of recorded sermons from hundreds of speakers.

Some years ago, Sheri and I were sitting in a conference in Canada listening to others speak while awaiting the time that I would take the pulpit. A new presenter I didn't know took the pulpit next. After greeting the crowd, he made some statements that seemed familiar to me.

"Sheri," I whispered, "he's telling Howard Hendricks' stories." She "shushed" me and kept focusing on the message, trying to enjoy the richness of its content. But I grew increasingly uncomfortable as the well-worn groove in my mind alerted me to the speaker's plagiarism.

"Sheri," I whispered again, "his next story is going to be about a man in prison." Her head swiveled, and she looked at me when the preacher launched into a story about a man in prison. This presenter had not only completely stolen another preacher's ideas, right down to the preacher's personal stories, but in so doing violated one of the cardinal rules of communication: He was predictable.

When our listeners predict what we will say or do, we are operating in the lowest form of communication. Years ago, Sheri and I attended a church where, on the second hymn and the second verse, we would be asked to stand in the auditorium. The order of the worship service was so predictable that people went through the motions mechanically but checked out mentally.

I challenge you to mix things up! What verse of Scripture states that you even have to preach a different sermon each week? One pastor friend preached the same sermon several times in a row to illustrate that before the people moved forward "in truth," they needed to learn the previous truth. People become disengaged with what is always done the same way. "Mixing things up," does not mean confusion but creativity.

First, get focused. The most effective presenters are those who know the value of concentrating their resources on well-defined goals and objectives. We need to remind ourselves constantly that we are headed somewhere and want our people to go with us. It is common for individuals and organizations to attempt more than they can do because they fail to comprehend the big picture or grand design behind a project. When we are fifty miles away from a twenty thousand-foot mountain, we can conclude wrongly the amount of time, energy and resources required to climb to the summit. We have to focus on the challenges before us as we prepare to bring our presentations, ramp up in our thinking process and then roll out successfully the message to change lives forever. Our focus sustains power and momentum for the long run. If we do not focus, people begin asking why are we here and what are we trying to accomplish.

The practice of narrowing our field of focus is called "delimiting the scope of inquiry." We need to concentrate our creativity, resources and energies on just those tasks that must be done in order to succeed, and lead our team weekly in discussions to become more successful in our presentations. Our goal is not to keep things in chaos to be unpredictable, but to lead people into uncharted paths of learning and development.

THE FOUNDATION OF INCREASING COMMUNICATION

We need to teach people how to care, cooperate and create. You may wonder, "What does caring, cooperating and creating have to do with predictability?" Everything! The greater people mature in these areas, the more open they will be to newer and bigger ideas. They will also be more willing to address teachings from a new angle and "do church" in a more creative manner.

Caring

The tenacity to do the difficult comes when people feel deep concern for humanity's ills as well as humanity's promise. We must develop and demonstrate a caring attitude before our people. It is one thing to say that we care but much harder to demonstrate caring before the eyes of the people. "Those who genuinely care are highly sensitive to human needs, observing what should be done to correct problems while being guided by passion, dedication, commitment and the will to persevere." (Vance and Deacon, 65-66)

The deeper our listeners care about a particular subject, the more they will want to learn about it. The deeper the connect with our audience on a theme, the more creativity emerges to solve the problems relating to its fulfillment in people's lives. When our audience cares deeply about the same outcomes as us, the higher their listening. One of the foundational building blocks as a communicator is knowing what your audience wants to learn about and what they are deeply committed to.

The tenacity to do the difficult comes when people feel deep concern for humanity's ills as well as humanity's promise.

Cooperating

The monumental leadership transformation taking place throughout the world has introduced a more collaborate effort among church staffs. Team-based leadership is the direct result of people realizing that most of the problems before us are so large that no single person alone can solve them. This is not only true in the work place but also in the local church. More pastors are realizing that the weekly demands placed upon the minister can hinder the effectiveness of the weekly presentations. "There is so much knowledge and information available today about what should be done to prosper that no one person is smart enough to act in isolation. It is more than just a desire for collaborative work habits." (Vance and Deacon, 66-67) In some churches, pastors assign their people to teams without showing how these teams will cooperate with each other for particular outcomes. If we fail to show the end zone, the temptation will be for teams to attempt to outperform each other without making greater progress on the big picture. Our goal is not to "do church" better but to communicate the Gospel more effectively with a result that we win more souls to Christ!

The greater the commitment, the greater the cooperation. The overarching reason why some churches possess a cooperative spirit is a compelling vision to which key leaders have committed themselves. When people are committed to each other through common vision, they are more apt to permit creative changes to take place in the worship service. Once that is accomplished, negative comments from negative people are minimized by their own lack of team spirit.

The higher the unpredictability in a service or presentation, the higher the attention span. No matter what you do, cooperation and interaction with other humans and increasingly sophisticated technology is essential to the success of your creative license.

Creating
Creative people and organizations love changes. They love spontaneity. People become tired of sequels, copies and phonies. Invention, innovation, and originality are the lifeblood of any organization and keep stretching the local church. Authors Vance and Deacon have said:

> Creativity is especially personal. Individual people as well as entire organizations take on an identity based on their commitment to creativity. It may be subtle and understated but the degree to which we allow creativity to enrich our lives will rub off on those around us. Creativity

is anything but superficial. It represents the very core of who we are and why we do what we do. (Vance and Deacon, 70)

To increase our communication capacity, we need to create a foundation of genuine caring, cooperation and creativity.

THE FORMULA FOR INCREASING COMMUNICATION

When a leader wishes to mature positive attributes of a caring person, the secret is to get the person involved. We will "know" when we "go." I remember a presenter teaching on the subject of "fire in an organization." He brought a fireman to the platform. The fireman taught on the explosive nature of fire and made me feel as if I had been to a fire in real life. That presentation took place in the year of 1993, but I have never forgotten it.

Involvement

The greater the involvement, the greater the learning. While people are listening to your presentation, give ample reason for the listener to grow in their capabilities. We learn not just by knowing but by going, not just by hearing, but by helping. During and after your presentation encourage your listeners to become involved in this "real world" where people live and die, where people receive and reject Christ. There are many ways to achieve this: 1) Provide a checklist of opportunities; 2) Provide a live testimony of a person who illustrates what you have taught; and 3) Lead a group a people to show them how your teaching will work in the "real world."

Information

Teach your listeners about the changes and show them where you are going. The mind will not accept what it cannot understand. Knowledge and competence expand when people are informed. On the one hand, when people are constantly asked to do something, they usually end up resisting leadership or faking a cooperative attitude. On the other hand, those who are truly involved in the process and informed about what's going on in the organization are motivated to cooperate. Action without information is usually irresponsible.

One of our goals during our presentation is to open our listeners' minds to new and exciting realities. When they see how a certain set of facts impact their lives, the information will serve as a "what is in it for me?" reality. When our audience comprehends that the involvement and the information will truly help their lives, then updated motivation will keep them going. The more solid information that we provide to people the higher the believability of the audience of us and our message.

Inspiration

We tend to be most inspired by people who achieve noteworthy success and accomplish worthwhile objectives with their lives on behalf of others. Inspired leadership is applauded and often rewarded with recognition, money, influence or affection. It is a far wiser and more productive investment for everyone in your organization, from the top down, to learn creativity. We must make it a priority to nurture and mature inspirational leaders throughout our ministries.

Inspiration is the byproduct of active accomplishment. At our office, we keep a notebook out on a desk entitled, "Book of Wins." Every team member is encouraged to record in it each accomplishment we make that inches us toward our goal. Of course, we are grateful for the big wins, but life is usually lived with the small ones that lead to big wins. Active accomplishments mostly take place in creative environments. Vance and Deacon challenge us:

> Becoming an inspirational leader means leading your people on a journey of discovery by charting a creative course where they also learn how to become self-motivated. Creativity thrives where people are inspired. (Vance and Deacon, 75)

We have discussed inspiration in other critical places throughout this book. Just keep in mind when you stand up in front of an audience the next time that they want to be involved, informed, and inspired.

THE FORECAST OF INCREASING COMMUNICATION

It is more about the people than the steeple. Our listeners want to know how your information fits in the big picture of real life.

People

People contribute and successfully solve problems when they have the skills needed to succeed in their environment. Training people how to think through challenges will help bring down problems and increase solutions. When our presentation helps a person to solve what he or she considers "the big problems" at home or work, the value of our messages exponentially grows practically overnight. The presenter with a testimony of proven results wins against a person with an argument of negativism that says "this is not possible or cannot be done." Do you want to persuade people? Bring presentations you have practiced in real life and garnered proven results.

Place

While preparing your presentations or messages, think carefully from every angle how you can bring more impact into the room. Think through the eyes of Googlers and Gutenbergers. There are times when the lighting needs to be adjusted for effect or people need to be greeted in a certain way as they arrive, all in preparation for the presentation. Sometimes the bulletins needed to be handed out early and in other instances it would be best to be given while the people are leaving the presentation. Engage the audience from different angles—from the senses to knowledge to application.

When I drove to my office this morning, I talked on the phone and thought about other things. I can do this because I know this path very well. However, the first time I drove to the office, I had to pay close attention because I had never been that way before. I travel between 45 to 48 weeks per year and know that I need to spend time thinking about the journey before I leave home. During our preparation of our presentation, we want to spend considerable time thinking through the various options and outcomes of our message, so our audience finds themselves on a new road where they have to pay close attention. When our listeners are in a stale environment that is not prone to be creative, their attention, and therefore their growth, is limited.

Every age group enjoys unplanned surprises. We do not want to turn our sacred services into a circus in the name creativity. Yet, Gutenbergers will enjoy meaningful changes, and Googlers will conclude that the preacher really wants to connect with them. What we want is not chaos or confusion, but a heightened tension in the presentation because people do not know what could be coming next, and are looking forward to a few surprises that will keep each presentation exciting and enjoyable.

For leaders to be able to predict certain outcomes is healthy and a high quality trait. For example, people need to know which way the front of the auditorium is, what time the presentation or gathering will begin and when it will end. But beyond that, most people simply will not grow until the creative process touches their lives.

America celebrates its birthday on July 4, our Independence Day. I had the rare privilege of being in our home church for Sunday morning service. It was a great day to be there, because one of America's founding fathers, Benjamin Franklin, interrupted the pastor's sermon to talk about our nation. The costume looked authentic, the conversation was funny, the presentation was unexpected, original, captivating, and entirely unpredictable. Even though he knew the holiday weekend congregation would be smaller, the pastor still made his presentation the best it could be. What a memorable mark he made on us!

The lowest form of communication is predictability. The highest form of communication is the lack of predictability. When predictability is too high, then communication is too low. Balance brings believability.

Left Brain
(Principles/Rational)

Right Brain
(Pictures/Relational)

LAW

17

THE POLISH IS IN THE TRANSITION

The elders who rule well are to be considered worthy of double honor, especially those who work hard at preaching and teaching. (1 Tim 5:17)

My daughter Olivia and I love to watch fireworks. Although she is only eight years old, we have managed to see enough fireworks displays that Olivia has acquired an eye for the best. Some fireworks shows just pop-pop-pop in sequence and are beautiful but a bit boring. Others have smaller bursts, then large multiple bursts that illumine the sky with giant flowers that rain down oceans of tiny sparks in ever-changing patterns of dazzling color. The pyrotechnicians who produce the most masterful fireworks displays are those who time and sequence the grand displays of light, interspersed with smaller brilliant bursts of color.

I cannot think of any area of life that is not filled with transitions and phases in order to move forward and upward. It seems like yesterday that I sat in a fourth grade class listening to a teacher explain how to create an outline. As she demonstrated the outline on the chalkboard, it became clear to this ten-year-old boy that the transition from the "one" to the "two," and so on, made all of the difference in the world.

When the worship leader in the church services flows from one song to the next one, without making special announcements for the new chorus or hymn, you are observing someone who has mastered the art of successful transitions. It is the transitions built into the sermon that replace the roughness with smoothness.

The timed transition may come in different forms. As we move from the introduction to the body of the message to the conclusion, we build in transitional summary statements and illustrations to move the audience forward. Master the transitions in the message, and our hearers will stay with us.

One of the greatest lessons I ever learned about sermonic preparation is the difference between the "eye" and "ear." When we write sermons to be graded in seminary, the eye is used more than the ear so the professor may read it for the grade. For example, we are sure to have correct sentence structure to meet the scrutiny of the professor's eye. However, when it comes to writing sermons to be presented orally, we need to prepare for the "ear" more than eye. If the sermon does not "sound good," then people will not pay attention to it.

For years I have written my entire sermon out verbatim, listened to how it sounds to my ears, and then I go back through the entire message with highlighters. I use various markers for the main points, key summary statements, and pivotal illustrations, and I commit these elements to memory. Once I have gone through this process several times carefully, I am able to succinctly present the message and even shorten it based upon time constraints. The less we add "fill-ins" due to the lack of preparation or understanding, the higher the appreciation our audience has for our message. Any minister who has been preaching for a number of years can preach an hour; but the master teacher is able to reduce it to a short, simple, powerful message.

Transitions glue the end of one section to the beginning of the next and provide a natural flow from one key element to another. But their most important job is to build interest throughout the presentation. Transitions are like the lock mechanism that connects the cars on a train and then pulls them along in the same direction.

USE TRANSITIONS BETWEEN ALL IMPORTANT IDEAS

Transitions build bridges between our presentation's key points. Many presenters spend hours and hours developing their presentations, more hours rehearsing and even more hours getting the room ready. Then they negate all their work by failing to build and use careful transitions. Our presentations begin long before we speak the first word. The audience has sized us up long before we begin. In essence, many transitions have taken place before the power point slide is presented or the first word is spoken.

Listening is hard work for our audience. The quickest way for an audience to lose track is by failing to tell them where we are going. This is a big mistake! Audience members need signals and guideposts, just like travelers, to reassure them that they are on the right track and that it's worth their effort to continue down this road. Transitions in our presentations provide these mental guideposts. Transitions tell the audience that something new is coming and that the previous element of the presentation is coming to a close.

As a general rule, use a transition whenever you move from one major idea to another. It tells your audience that you are moving on, that you covered this "big idea" and are going to "big idea two." Usually a sentence or two will do. By planning and writing these in advance, you can avoid the problem many presenters have in forgetting to use transitions at all. This is an easy mistake to make in the excitement of the presentation. Without transitions, there is little sequencing of thoughts for the hearer.

When your audience looks like they don't know where you or they are going, this is not a good sign! Point them in the right direction and go there together. Transitions act like stairways in the presentation you are building. They step listeners up from one key point to the next. They are a minute but critical piece of a presentation. Transitions help your listeners stay with you, making your message easier to follow and to remember.

As the presenter, you know when you are moving on—when you are stepping up from the first floor and proceeding to the second. But your audience does not have this information. Without transitions, you could be halfway into your next step, and your listeners still think they are back on step one. They are lost trying to figure out which way is up or down and conclude that you were unprepared, unorganized or simply unclear. Or, if you lose your listeners at the point of the transition, your audience could feel they are not prepared enough for your message and will simply give up.

Transitions help keep the audience on track. They also serve to bring the audience back. If some people have mentally wandered elsewhere, a transition can regain their attention. It alerts people that your message is advancing.

There is no excuse for a presenter to overlook transitions, since they are so simple to devise. Transitions are simple statements that act as a mini-summary and mini-preview within the body of a presentation. It announces the end of one step or element and introduces the next.

USE TRANSITIONS TO INTRODUCE AND SUM UP NEW IDEAS, ACTIVITIES OR EVEN BEFORE TAKING A BREAK

With the explosion of muti-media software, the creative possibilities for presentations have never been better. Even when it comes to developing transitions, it is easy to project pictures or words on screens without saying a word. We need to remember that the visual element is stronger than the vocal and verbal elements.

Transitions should be used to open the door to a new idea or thought so the listener knows something new has come his or her way. Remember, the mind craves order, and our minds repel what is confusing or does not make sense. The listener will not normally take the time to figure this out. It is the presenter's responsibility to deliver the thoughts in a meaningful, sequential order.

When the idea is completed or the thought has been presented, it is important to close the door that was opened to demonstrate information flow for the minds of your hearers. The masterful communicator knows how to bring a powerful close to a thought and "barely introduce" the new idea before taking a break. This keeps the creative tension, between the audience knowing too much and not knowing enough. This is the creative balance needed to pull the listeners close to us.

Keep Transitions Short And Sweet

When we enter into a transition, this is not the time to mention a thought that we had previously forgotten. This will only bring confusion, rather than forward motion. Everyone enjoys going on an exciting trip or journey. When the road is simple with sweetness to go with it, the more fun the participants have along the way.

Imagine a transition this way. You are taking the train into New York City from Long Island. When you get to Jamaica Station, you will have to transition from one train to another. Yet all along the way, the announcer is reminding you of the next stops. The announcer tells you where you are and where you are going.

Your audience should never lose sight of where they are and where they are going, but be careful not to give too much information too fast. It is important to keep the creative tension throughout the presentation. What makes a book a "page-turner" is the fact that the tension pulls the reader into the story and propels the reader forward.

The transition is the key to keep the movement moving from one section to the next. In fact, the transitions should become so smooth that the listeners do not even recognize the transitions during the learning experience. (Jeary, 192)

USE ATTENTION-GETTING STATEMENTS, RELATIVE STATISTICS AND HUMOR

Sometimes the power of just one word can electrify an audience when spoken at the right second. As every other part of the sermon, transitions are wrapped up in the correct timing. It is important for the presenter to know when he or she has given enough information, then tie it together in a pungent transition, before moving on.

Between seven to eight minutes on average, there is a television commercial during a scheduled program. Whether we realize it or not, we have programmed our attention spans to be about that long. Even though as presenters we may not necessarily appreciate this teaching fact, it is noteworthy to remember that we consistently have to awaken our listeners to keep them mentally engaged. Dynamic transitions properly positioned in programmed intervals will help us lead our audience through to the end.

If you choose to use statistics as transitions, be sure to project them on the screen. The average mind cannot digest numbers without "paper" or without seeing them at the same time. The right statistic can be dramatic and cause your audience to want more and more information throughout your message. Learn to develop a particular style in your presentations and your audience will come to realize when you are transitioning from one major thought to another one.

Vary Your Transitions

There are unlimited creative ways to give transitions and move your audience forward. With the digital age, we can use sound or video clips, pictures, verbal statements combined with pictures on a screen and more. Use different kinds of transitions, even during just one presentation. Study the transitions of notable presenters to witness how world class presenters utilize many different transition types. The transitions become so natural that experienced presenters do not even have to think much before they apply various transitions in their presentation.

Use Gestures And Body Movements

How many times do we see a police officer simply yelling directions at drivers? The police officer nearly always uses gestures because he or she knows we will only clearly understand if we can see something while at the same time hearing something.

When our gestures and body movements indicate that we are in transition from one thought to another thought or another step from the previous step, the impact of our presentation just went up considerably. For example, while we are briefly summarizing the previous thought, we can point toward the past. As we move our presentation to the next thought, we can point to the future.

A simple way of indicating transition is to walk to one place on our stage repeatedly when giving the brief summary of where we have been in the presentation and then walk toward the other side of the platform as we begin to share the next major thought or take the next big step forward in your presentation.

Some of us are old enough to remember the dial-up days of the Internet, and others are too young to remember high speed broadband. These two different approaches to getting on the Internet and staying on the Internet show us the importance of transitions in presentations. Whether the Internet user knows it or not, many transitions take place from one web page to another, one website to another. Yet, they are so seamless that we do not even recognize them. No one enjoyed the slow-ness of dial up but endured it. Yet, how many times do we say to ourselves when we are confused or things come slow, "Is this really worth it?" It is the clumsy transitions that make us ask the questions. When transi-tions are awkward or do not make sense, people become frustrated or even difficult to communicate to.

The masterful teacher makes transitions look seamless. When prac-ticing your presentation, be sure to practice the art of moving from one thought to the next, from one step to the next, while giving just enough information to keep the creative tension in place throughout your presentation.

| **Left Brain** | | **Right Brain** | |
| (Principles/Rational) | | (Pictures/Relational) | |

LAW

18

HUMOR IS THE QUICKEST WAY TO A PERSON'S HEART

A joyful heart is good medicine. (Pro 17:22)

Dr. Walter Kaiser is one of the world's all-time great theologians and Old Testament Bible scholars. His library in his office is literally "his," the books that he himself has written over years of study, preaching, teaching and presiding over some of the greatest seminaries in the world. With all his mental exertion, education, and erudition, I have been with Dr. Kaiser in conference after conference where he literally shocks his audiences with delightful jokes. Although sometimes corny and obviously rehearsed hundreds of times, his humor brings belly laughs. Why? Because he allows his audience to breathe! Even the great blue whale, the King of the Seas, has to come up for air once in a while.

When speaking of David and Goliath, for example, Dr. Kaiser tells of David making a "good impression" on Goliath, that David's perspective had never "entered Goliath's mind" before. He teases the audience with a question, "Do you know why David chose five stones?" Then he delivers a playful answer, "Neither do I, but most preachers have preached a sermon on the significance of the five." Here is a man who could teach us the entire Bible cover to cover, but he knows how much the mind can endure, and he punctuates his presentation with humor to help us grasp the truths.

This is sermonizing humor at its best because it brings the desired results. We do not tell jokes to fill time but to allow the minds of our audience members a necessary break. The masterful communicator uses all of the tools available, and humor is one of the most important ones. Make people laugh, and you will win their hearts.

Humor creates a special bond between you and your listeners. It is virtually impossible to dislike someone who makes us laugh, who helps us enjoy ourselves. A sense of humor makes us more genial, more warm, more likable. The strong, pleasurable emotions people associate with high spirits make your message enjoyable to listen to and memorable.

Our goal is not to simply tell jokes. Leave comedy to the comedians. How many people do you know tell really good jokes? Perhaps one person in a hundred is a good joke-teller. If our joke falls flat, we are going down with it. Persuasion screeches to a halt. Unless we are in that rare ninety-ninth percentile, who can actually tell a joke successfully, with timing, delivery and flair, we should simply leave that alone.

Fun is better than funny. Our goal is not *comedy* but *connection* that creates an atmosphere of openness, friendliness, growth and puts our listeners at ease.

Find the form of humor that works for you. What is your sense of humor like? What kind of humor do you use in your everyday conversation that could be applied in your presentation? Do you have a gift for seeing the humor in everyday life? Do you have seemingly off-the-cuff comments that make people laugh? Do you have the ability to remember funny statements or humorous historic quotes made by others? It was said that even the comedienne Lucille Ball was not a funny person naturally, but she had applied herself to learn comedic timing and became one of the funniest people in television history.

While I speak, I constantly think ahead of when I will need to bring the audience up for air. If I sense or see uneasiness with the audience, I will bring a humorous element into the presentations sooner. We can use humor in language. The right emphasis of a single word can provoke a laugh and cement the connection between you and your listener.

There are some ways that we can grow in our humor. We need to learn to think funny and look at things from different angles. Humor is the hardest communication skill to exercise so it needs to become a mindset. Begin to look for humor all around you. There is even laughter at funerals that can be appropriate. People love to laugh. They like to be with people who are lighthearted. Think of those who make you laugh and feel lighthearted.

> *Fun is better than funny. Our goal is not comedy but connection that creates an atmosphere of openness, friendliness, growth and puts our listeners at ease.*

We need to think funny, and we need to think friendly. This is also a mindset. The next person you see, think of being friendly rather than ignoring the person. With a friendly mindset, humor and humanization are much more likely to occur. It becomes a habit.

Until you have matured in your presentations, write down your humor. Since this is a difficult skill to master, write down humorous elements until you learn the best ways to develop humor in your life and in your presentations. Keep a journal or diary of observations and funny quotations, anecdotes, and stories. When keeping a story diary, it is not necessary to write down the entire story. Just jot down the trigger words or thoughts to bring it back to mind. Keep a file of anecdotes people send you or copy pages with humor in them that you find in magazines and books.

Study communicators to see how they work humor into their presentations. Those who are the best communicators know how to weave humor to the point that if you are not paying close attention, you will not even notice how they do it.

When speaking overseas or in a different culture, humor is much harder to master than in our own culture. When I travel, I share a humorous element from my presentation with those around me prior to speaking. If the person who lives in that culture or the translator does not laugh, I quickly remove it from the actual live presentation! When we are just learning to understand an audience, a failed attempt to engage our hearers in laughter is one of the most embarrassing things we could ever do.

RELEASE TENSION IN PEOPLE'S HEARTS AND MINDS

Simply put, humor helps to eliminate stress. The Bible says, "Laughter is like medicine." As we continue to develop our presentations over time, one of our overarching goals is to pull people close to us, especially during presentations. I have a strong conviction that when people come to listen to my presentation, they should leave refreshed and not worn out. When we give our presentations, even when they are dealing with a complex or difficult subject, our presence should make the room brighter instead of darker. Have you have felt worn out after being in someone's presence? Have you ever felt refreshed when you have been with someone else?

Stress continues to rise in our world. Our listeners should not just relax during our presentation but also release the tension in their hearts and minds. One metaphor that may help us to understand this concept is the popularity of the fifteen-minute massage. As I travel, I find in shopping malls or airports those brief massages we can receive out in the open while other travelers or shoppers walk by. The goal of massage is to release stress and get the knots out of our muscles.

During our presentations, we can help our listeners to release their stress through humor that is creatively interwoven through our time together. When our muscles relax, they stop pulling our bones in the wrong direction. When we help to release tension in our listeners' minds, their thoughts will eventually stop being pulled into self-defeating patterns.

This is not to say that we cannot talk about anything negative or uncomfortable during our presentations. Just the opposite. When we learn to apply humor in the most constructive manner possible, it also gives us greater opportunity to discuss what could otherwise be uncomfortable. Learning to develop "laughing moments" in a presentation does not mean that one does not understand the seriousness of overall presentation or the surrounding situations that an audience may be confronting at the moment. In the midst of every storm or challenge, people need an opportunity to be human and to simply be able to laugh at themselves or with the presenter.

Many years ago Sheri and I lost our first child, Jennifer. Jennifer was born early and lived in the hospital for six weeks before dying in Sheri's arms. We had to find laughter and humor in our lives even while walking through "the valley of the shadow of death." Of course, we needed more than humor to sustain us, but we did learn how to laugh even in a most difficult time.

When we learn to apply humor in the most constructive manner possible, it also gives us greater opportunity to discuss what could otherwise be uncomfortable.

During Jennifer's brief illness and after her death, I continued to travel and give presentations to people everywhere. Then, seven years later, I found myself doing the same after the untimely and unexpected death of our son, James. When I began a presentation, I did not spend the first ten minutes telling people how bad life was or how we should give up our hopes and dreams when hurtful things comes to our lives. I brought the Gospel of hope and healing even while being transparent about our grief.

Every time we stand to give a presentation, our audience is filled with hurting people. They do not need to be reminded of how difficult life can be. When people see a smile on my face or hear laughter in my voice, even when they realize our family has buried two children, they receive a strong message: Laughter truly is a way of healing broken hearts and helping people to live life again. If we wish for our listeners to get close to us and connect, there has to be humor, mixed with hope in our lives. This does not mean that we cultivate a "fake it until we make it" mentality or presentation. Even though we live

Every time we stand to give a presentation, our audience is filled with hurting people. They do not need to be reminded of how difficult life can be.

in a real world, we simply choose to believe that "winners do not reflect on what they are going through but where they are going to."

REFUEL PEOPLE SO THEY CAN DIVE DEEP
WITH YOU AGAIN

One morning when our family was vacationing in Maui during the early 1990s, I was taking a walk along the beach with my video camera. While I was recording the beautiful blue ocean in the waters that connect Molokai, Lanai, and Maui, a large whale came bursting breach out of the water and made a gigantic splash. A few moments later, this whale did it again. He or she was breathtakingly beautiful, but it also just looked like this giant was having fun!

Laughter truly is a way of healing broken hearts and helping people to live life again.

Our listeners need to come up for mental air, so they can stay emotionally alert. Otherwise, if the teaching is too dense or heavy, they will simply give up. If we do not master the skill that provides some breathing time, we will wear them out before achieving our presentation outcomes.

Once the listeners catch their breath, there is willingness to dive deep again with us. With each dive, they become more confident in us that we will not hold them down too long or go too deep. Humor gives them the space they need to allow their minds to rest their mental muscles. Master communicators learn when to dive again and when to come up for air.

REFRESH THE AUDIENCE MEMBERS AND
OPEN THEIR MINDS TO NEW THOUGHTS

Once our presentation has stretched people's minds, there will be more room for larger thoughts in the future. When people leave our presentations, they should believe that there is hope for them. Humor is a door that opens peoples' hearts to laugh even in dark and difficult days. Remember the people who are hurting so bad that they feel it will not be acceptable for them to laugh. Your ability to laugh at the right things will help them to laugh again, even when they hurt inside.

Humor provides a "pause" in a presentation for the mind to reflect over what has just been taught, both the listener's mind and your mind.

It gives a small but powerful space for the listener to think. Waiting time is not necessarily wasted time. The mind thinks at the speed of life and can come to serious conclusions in a matter of a second or two. When we give people a moment to think, they will be able to make small decisions along the way regarding what you are saying and then make the "big decision" at the end. The big decision is the ability to make the necessary changes as a result of your presentation.

REMIND THEM THAT THE PRESENTER IS HUMAN AND ENJOYS LIFE

For a presenter to be believed, we must be believable. The endorsement of our spouses and children "closes the sale" most of the time for the listener to "buy into" what we are saying. Showing pictures or telling stories about a family outing or a special moment endears the audience to us. From time to time I purposefully mention my family and share a humorous story from my personal life.

Yet, there needs to be balance. If we speak too much of our family or use too many family anecdotes, our audience may think we are more interested in talking about our family than providing rock solid solutions to their everyday challenges at work or home. Also, most children do not want to be at the center of their parent's presentations. It is wise to go over your comments with the family first and even, in some instances, to obtain permission to use a story.

We live in a broken world, and families come under heavy attack. If we are going to speak about most subjects and yet our families are falling apart, people may wonder what is wrong with our life. Can the presenter be trusted if his or her family is falling apart?

Humor provides a "pause" in a presentation for the mind to reflect over what has just been taught, both the listener's mind and your mind. It gives a small but powerful space for the listener to think.

Yet, just because a person's family does fall apart does not always mean that the presenter is less than adequate to bring a powerful presentation. The trust level is simply much higher when the presenter is able to show a picture and speak of the family in glowing terms. There is something about a family that sticks together through thick and thin that challenges others to keep pressing on.

One last warning is that when you incorporate humorous anecdotes, make sure that they are not made at the expense of a segment of your audience. If you do, you could very well lose the most important person in your audience and not know it.

Humor is a tremendous skill even though it takes some time for most of us to master. Once humor has become part of our presentations, we will find ourselves being able to pull people closer to us and to close the gap between them and us.

Left Brain
(Principles/Rational)

Right Brain
(Pictures/Relational)

LAW

19

THE FIRST NINETY SECONDS
ARE THE MOST IMPORTANT

But Peter, along with John, fixed his gaze on him and said,
"Look at us!" And he began to give them his attention,
expecting to receive something from them. (Acts 3:4-5)

At a recent Southern Baptist Convention, I was privileged to join some friends who were speaking and seven thousand pastors gathered to hear a series of electrifying messages led by two-time president Johnny Hunt. I was surprised when the program shifted on the second afternoon from well-known dignitaries to a young pastor who looked scarcely old enough to have completed seminary. As the young pastor took the podium, audience members shifted in their seats. I realized I was not alone in wondering what qualified this person for this stage. I was even more surprised when, like a professional, he took the stage and set the table within ninety seconds.

"I don't come with a big church," is the way I remember him starting. "I don't have a best-selling book, a TV show, or a national ministry. I don't have fame or notoriety. I come to you with only one thing. The only thing I have that qualifies me to speak to you is this Bible right here."

With that, he held up his Bible and captivated his audience. Where he was going from there was unpredictable. It was a great start! Every eye was riveted from that moment forward.

You have crafted a message, anticipated the outcomes, planned the invitation, polished the transitions, but before you start, you need to consider *how* you start. There are nearly limitless ways to begin a message, but the strategic goal remains the same. We must capture the attention and arouse interest immediately or face losing the audience. We must view the introduction not in terms of what begins the presentation, but in terms of what will open up the audience. The purpose of an introduction is to invite people into the arena of ideas with us. If we fail to open the hearts and minds of our audience, we will fail to persuade them to our point of view or to activate them to apply a particular action.

While you are preparing the first ninety seconds, think carefully about the characteristics of the people you are trying to persuade. Develop a snapshot of your audience. Answer questions like:

1. Gender?
2. Age?
3. Occupation and profession?
4. Educational level?
5. Setting?
6. Mood and expectations?

Once we have identified the predominant characteristics of the audience and the setting, we ask ourselves: What will appeal to them? What will this group consider to be important? What will be meaningful and memorable for my listeners in these circumstances?

We answer the following questions, to prepare to get the audience on the train of thought with us for the entire time:

1. What is the most relevant way or method to the subject and to the audience?
2. What is most appropriate to the setting?
3. What best suits my own personal style so I can begin comfortably and naturally?

If the presenter does not capture the attention of the congregation at the very beginning of the sermon, the audience may never enter into the heart and soul of the sermon. People today are quick studies. They reach judgments faster than the previous generation.

WARMING UP THE AUDIENCE

A leading presenter in the United States, Ron Hoff states:

> Warming up an audience simply means to soften the strangeness, defuse the defenses and slice through the natural reluctance to expose feelings and emotions openly... .There is an art to unfrost an audience while moving quickly into our introduction. It is like an emotional massage, coaxing the face to smile, the senses to respond, the arterial system to open up. (Hoff, 37).

The audience will reflect the attitude and manner of the presenter. As you sow, you shall reap! Though at times uncomfortable, we have to learn how to get into our presentation and feel it in our hearts, while at the same warming our listeners. There are at least two things, according Hoff, we can do in the first ninety seconds to make a big difference.

Focus on a Friend

By "friend," this does not necessarily mean that you personally know the person. It means that it is obvious that this individual is excited about the prospect of this presentation and is supporting you. Hoff fine tunes this with:

> Focus on someone who is committed to your support. This must be a legitimate member of the audience who is not a member of your hand-picked team. Once you have established contact with your one, true friend—lock in. Let the eye contact register. Let that person know by your manner that he or she is very important, and that from that moment on, you and this person are going to develop a relationship during your message. Your goal is not just to build a case before your listeners but to build a relationship with everyone in the room. (Hoff, 38-39)

I don't speak Spanish. When I was in Argentina recently to bring a presentation to approximately twenty key leaders, I "focused on a friend." I mentioned one particular leader present who was a "spiritual father" to many of the leaders in the meeting. I recognized him before the others, mentioned our many occasions when we had previously met, and asked him to say something. His comments brought validity to the Billion Soul Network and convinced all persons in the meeting that they needed to participate in the upcoming Summit that I was about to discuss. This is warming up an audience!

Once you have made one friend in the audience, you can move on to another person and then to another. Your audience is warmed up even though only seconds have gone by. It is important to show or demonstrate confidence by making eye contact and building connections in the room from the very beginning.

Say Something That You Really Enjoy

Say what is easy to relate that is also relevant. There should be a pleasantness about your spirit and your words before the audience. When people sense that you truly enjoy what you are doing and what you are saying, they are more likely to enjoy the entire presentation.

Warming up an audience can be done within your first ninety seconds. Just start making friends, and talking in a way that comes easily and naturally for you.

There are simple steps to building the bridge between the presenter and the listeners:

THE ROAD TO RAPPORT

Most audiences want the speaker to succeed. Even a negative audience has a vested interest in our success. The more successful we are, the more they will enjoy our message. Every audience loves three things:

- Respect
- Rapport
- Entertainment

Public speaking expert Tony Jeary highlights the above three in "Inspire Any Audience," and further states: "These three elements provide a threshold for audience buy-in, involvement and satisfaction. The first words out of our mouths should convince the audience that we will, above all else, deliver these three audience imperatives" (Jeary, 85).

According to Jeary, "The way to guarantee an audience's commitment and loyalty is to involve them in our presentation…. The key to audience buy-in is to make them part owner of the presentation… Once the audience has taken part ownership of the presentation, they will be sure not to let us fail" (Jeary, 86). Even though they may not realize it you have a built a bridge of rapport with them and they will want to learn all they can from you. Some bridge-building steps include meeting as many attendees as possible before the presentation and starting your presentation on time.

We must prove that we are prepared for the presentation. Nothing sends the message that we don't care like being unprepared. Every detail counts—starting on time, having the appropriate materials ready and knowing what we are going to say. If our audience members sense that we are unprepared, they will quickly tune us out! Building rapport is critical for achieving audience buy-in. (Jeary, 86)

Awakening the Audience

Starting with, "Good morning, ladies and gentlemen" is the oldest opening in any speaker's repertoire. It is comfortable but boring. Instead of opening with a statement that most of the audience will simply ignore, we should begin with something that really grabs attention. It could be a quote or news that is positive. It does not have to be humorous. It should not have any words that are hard to pronounce or theories that are hard to digest. It should roll right out of your mouth. Some ministers create a trademark opening remark. Oral Roberts' was generally, "Something good is going to happen to you," and Kathryn Kuhlman's was, "I believe in miracles." The opening comments do not have to be outrageous, but attention-grabbing. Some suggestions:
- Begin with a startling statistic.
- Begin with a proactive question.
- Tell a story about something that recently happened to you.
- Refer to a current newsworthy event. (Jeary, 90)

Creating Credibility

"Credibility is bestowed upon us by others. It might come as the result of hard work but unless others give us credit for our work, we cannot gain credibility" (103). Here are some keys to demonstrating credibility:

Be Consistent—We have already discussed that audiences can see through pretension immediately, and it doesn't take long to see through other forms of dishonesty. We can be sure that the audience gets a sense of our integrity by:

Telling The Truth—Word upon word and precept upon precept, build a strong foundation—properly-checked facts, correct references, thorough preparation.

Add a personal story or two that further establishes your credentials; but never come across as bragging or superior.

Being Yourself—Trying to be someone we are not is almost as bad as telling a lie.

Staying Consistent—If we say we are starting at 8:30, then start at 8:30. If we say we will take frequent breaks, then we have frequent breaks.

Speak with passion—Say it like we mean it and our audience will believe our words.

Never pretend to know the answer to a question and never fake it—It is better to say "I don't know" and then find the answer (Jeary, 104).

Be Credentialed—We do not have to be experts before we can have expertise. Experts are people who have spent their lives learning about a certain subject. I have known many experts who understand Greek, Hebrew, Latin and German but who are dryer than dust and deader that King Tut. Just because a man is an expert does not mean that people want to listen to him. Experts can in fact alienate the audience and make the audience trust them less without even knowing it.

Regardless of who we are, we can improve our expertise by:

Understanding all sides of our subject—Preparing with care what we will and will not say.

Studying through the subject completely—When working with a new subject, do research before standing in front of an audience. Be ready for the tough questions!

Speaking the language of your audience—Learning some new terms the audience knows.

I have been accused of different things in my life, but have never been accused of knowing too much!

Be Contagious—If we are glad to be in front of the room, most listeners will be glad to have us there. Enthusiasm shows confidence and brings focus to our listeners. Within seconds people will make a decision as to whether or not you will be enjoyable to them. Remember that we decide on emotion and justify with facts later. Be sure to include eye contact throughout the room and not just a select few to make emotional connections.

Be Compassionate—"Convince our listeners that we understand how things look from their perspective. Prove it by letting them know we are there for them and not for ourselves" (Jeary, 107). The audience knows that I am a real person when they see a smiling face and a positive attitude even when knowing I have had heart-wrenching challenges. Having said this, however, do not bring excuses into your presentation as to why you not had enough time to prepare more for this presentation. Nearly everyone is busy and will not appreciate you thinking your busyness is more important than their valuable time.

Involve Your Influence

"Believable people know they are believable. We have to convince ourselves of our own credibility before we can convince others" (Jeary, 108). Like many people, I find it difficult to talk about my successes. Yet, if I do not say anything, then people do not know what God has done for me.

Our influence can be increased by sharing personal stories of accomplishments. Most introductions are inadequate. If our introduction as a guest speaker is inadequate, we can weave in some excellent facts in a discreet manner. We should not, however, wait too long lest people conclude wrongly that we are not qualified to address them. Our audience judges based upon depth of knowledge, personal experiences, level of preparedness, enthusiasm, appearance, and body language.

"It might be hard for you to make yourself believe that you have the right to be in front of the room. You must come right out and tell the audience why you have the right to be front of them" (Jeary, 110). This right is achieved by giving your personal experience, your knowledge and skill level and your credentials. Obviously, lying about credentials means your audience will never believe another word. When listing your credentials, a few important accomplishments is more than adequate. The goal is to earn trust quickly in the eyes and minds of your listeners.

Analyze the Atmosphere

The tone we establish determines how the audience perceives us. If they approve, we can expect nearly 100 percent buy-in. Everything counts when we are establishing tone. We need to know how to create the right atmosphere. It is good to create a conversational tone since people love conversing with each other. Our audience responds to emotion. We need to make sure that everything we say and do works both intellectually and emotionally.

The right tone is usually established successfully when we take the time to think through the small details, as well as the most obvious ones. Tone can be set for us, without our ever knowing it, if we do not attend to details. For example, if we do not study the confirmed list of attendees at a conference or banquet, it is possible for a very important person to be left off the list. We can have an embarrassment created for us by a host at the door saying something like, "I am sorry you are not on the list. If you would like to pay, then we can let you in."

Some may dismiss this as not being important, but my experience warns not to underestimate how others can set the tone, without our even knowing it. The experienced presenter knows that the tone is being established even before the first word of the presentation has been given. In everything we do, we seek to apply excellence, not perfection. Apply thoughtfulness, not chance. Apply timeliness, not randomness. The beginning of our presentation is some of the most important seconds of our lives.

Left Brain
(Principles/Rational)

Right Brain
(Pictures/Relational)

LAW

20

GIVE MORE THAN PEOPLE EXPECT TO RECEIVE

*So with many other exhortations he preached the gospel
to the people. (Lk 3:18)*

In the middle of the Sermon on the Mount, Jesus said, "Whoever forces you to go one mile, go with him two" (Mt 5:41). It is the "second mile" principle that will put a smile on our face, a spring in our step, and a song in our heart. The first mile is the "trial mile," and the second mile is the "smile mile." The key to living life with a smile is a Christ-centered life. It has been said, "A person wrapped up in himself makes a very small package." It is generally the extra 10 percent that ultimately makes the big difference in life and ministry.

Gutenbergers and Googlers alike know when their expectations have been met or exceeded. Aside from the constant presence of critics, we are to present in such a way that it can never be said we over-promised or under-performed. Let us be "second mile" preachers every time we step to the podium, lectern or pulpit!

Among the many grand and glorious principles taught by Jesus Christ, the principle of the "second mile" showcases the dynamics of true discipleship. The second mile is *the character mile*. What was Jesus talking about when He said, "And whoever shall force you to go one mile, go with him two"? In Jesus' day, the Romans had a practice that they had learned from the Persians about six hundred years earlier. This practice was to subjugate a people who had been conquered through war.

If a Roman soldier saw a Jewish man or boy, he could command the man or boy to carry his backpack or burden for a mile. The Roman mile is the same distance as our mile today. The Jewish boy or man was required by law to carry this soldier's burden for a mile. Most Jews would not carry this burden one inch or one foot further than the law required because of their resentment toward the Roman government.

Can you imagine how the Jews felt when Jesus said, "Go the second mile?" No doubt, the audience said, "He must be jesting." "Does he really expect us to do more than the law requires us to do?" In essence, Jesus was saying that his disciples need to do more than the legalists who do no more than what is required of them.

What is the principle of the second mile? It is to do more than is required or expected of us. Jesus is saying that any pagan or unsaved person can go one mile (Mt 5: 46-47). The first mile is to love those who love us. The second mile is to love those who do not love us. We must always remember that life is lived on three levels. The *hellish level* is to return evil for good. The *human level* is to return good for good and evil for evil. The *heavenly level* is to return good for evil. The second mile is to return good for evil.

When a Jewish man or boy is carrying the soldier's backpack for the first mile, he is a slave. However, when he chooses to carry the burden for a second mile, he then takes control of the situation. The character mile moves us from slaves to masters. The first mile is the "have to" mile, but the second mile is the "want to" mile.

In ministry today, we are expected to do more with less and go farther in a shorter amount of time. The expectations that people place on us at times can be most demanding. The key to a victorious attitude is to learn to rise above demands in our spirit and not allow small thinking to get us down. When we choose to go the extra mile, we may become fearful, wondering if anyone will go with us. Yet, our example on the second mile will inspire more than we have ever imagined. Regarding our presentations, we want to take our second mile attitude and always strive to give more than what is required.

Secondly, the second mile is the *commitment mile*. We go the first mile out of legalism but continue the second mile out of love. In order to live like Jesus, we must go the second mile when we experience *personal degradation* (Mt 5: 38-39). The first mile is to give place to revenge, but the second mile is to give place to love. Jesus said, "If someone slaps you on your right cheek, turn to him the other also." In order for someone to smite us on the right cheek it means that someone hit us with the back of the hand. Has someone treated you disrespect-fully? The best way to get rid of an enemy is to make a friend out of him.

In ministry today, we are expected to do more with less and go farther in a shorter amount of time.

There are times in life in general and in ministry in particular when others will disappoint us. I had to undergo a two-year period of time when I was smitten on my right cheek in ways that were shocking. In the natural, I wanted to set the record straight. It is during such times in ministry that we have the opportunity to preach our greatest presen-tations. People are watching to see how we live our lives and they are listening to our spirits, not just our substance. In those seasons we have to preach more than ever with compassion and not criticism. True spiritual discipline is not to step down but to help others step up! Once a leader has stepped down to argue and debate, he or she loses more leadership ground than one may realize. Higher thinking requires higher ground.

Furthermore, the commitment mile includes *personal defeat* (Mt 5:40). Jesus is talking about a legal settlement. In this legal matter, there is a brother who has been found guilty. He has been required to give his shirt. Jesus is saying, if you know you have done wrong, do not simply try to rectify the wrong by fulfilling the law, but go the second mile. If you are wrong, then apologize, get right with your brother and God, and go the second mile.

Not only does the second mile include personal degradation and personal defeat, but also *personal dedication* (Mt 5:42). We are to have a giving spirit. We are not simply to pay our bills, but give to those who are in need. In order to live like Jesus, we go the second mile when others have wronged us, when we have wronged others, and also when there are serious financial needs. We are not simply to convey a message but to find creative applications to drive a truth home.

As leaders, we are called to lead the way in generous giving. While traveling, I have observed that more than half of the pastors during the receiving of the offering, actually give an offering in front of the congregation. People are watching how we respond, to see whether or not we are truly leading the way in every level of our lives. We need to place a tithe or offering in the plate in each service. As a result of our leadership, in time, our weekly giving increases.

Third, the second mile is the *commission mile*. I have been working with people long enough to observe that highly successful people live by the second mile principle. The first mile is crowded but the second mile is not busy at all.

Imagine two different scenes with me. In the first scene, a Roman soldier commands a Jewish man or boy to carry his backpack or burden for an entire mile. The first Jewish male becomes extremely upset as he picks up the soldier's burden and begins to carry it. As he carries the backpack, he talks in angry tones to the soldier. At the end of a mile, he throws the burden down and returns home, full of rage, hatred, and anger.

The second scene is the complete opposite of the previous scene. As soon as the Roman soldier commands the man to carry his burden, the man responds with a warm Christian greeting. In his heart, he truly wants to win this soldier to Jesus Christ. Along the way, he encourages conversation between himself and the soldier. At the end of the first mile, the man says, "If you do not mind, I would be honored to carry your burden for a second mile."

Can you imagine the incredulous look on the soldier's face when he hears these words? The Roman soldier says, "There is something different about you. Most men become angry when I command them to carry my backpack. What makes you different from the others? The man says, "On one occasion, I heard Jesus Christ teach on the second mile principle. So, I am doing what Jesus Christ commanded me to do." The soldier responds, "Who is Jesus Christ?" The man answers, "He is the Messiah and savior of the world." By the time they reach the end of the second mile, this man has shared the gospel with this Roman soldier.

The second mile is the witnessing mile. I am convinced that more souls would be saved if we lived our lives on the second mile. We have more than one billion Christians in the world today. At the rate of the spread of Christianity, the first billion was the trial mile and the second billion will be the smile mile. Jesus went the second mile for all of us. Why would anyone want to sit with the critics when they could sit with the champions? Why would anyone want to live on the trial mile when we can live on the smile mile? Let's run the second mile together!

If we are determined to give a little extra or to polish the words a little more, then a compounding effect will happen in our lives. People know when they have heard a message that has been prayed over and well-prepared before they arrived at church. When we live this kind of prepared life, then we are ready when life's greatest challenges come our way. As we consistently invest into our spiritual and ministerial bank accounts, we will begin to live out of the overflow of our heart, knowledge, and experiences. Living the second mile in ministry prepares us for unplanned challenges or ministry opportunities.

For me, the ultimate test came due to something that most ministers will deal with to one degree or another—a cataclysmic event. When these come our way, we are called upon to step up to the highest level possible.

On September 11, 2001, the Trade Towers in New York City came crashing down, and our world changed forever. I was in Detroit, Michigan. I will never forget that afternoon when the late Dr. Bill Bright arranged a nationwide conference call with notable Christian leaders. The call had a "who's who" in Christian leadership, no need to name them. I felt honored just to be on the call, and somewhat comforted while the entire nation was rocking from the blow of an evil enemy. I didn't have to say anything, just help put the call together and listen. Dr. Bright led a time of prayer followed by a time of discussion.

After about an hour or so of prayer and discussion, Dr. Bright asked if I were still on the phone, and I responded that I was. Then he said something that would send chills down any expositor's back. He asked me to prepare a sermon to provide biblical understanding of the times and a challenge for the Church. He asked that I prepare it that night, so the next morning these leaders could review it, and then they would send it out to all their pastors and ministers across the nation for Sunday services.

This would be one of the greatest tests for any sermon-writer, ever. I literally could not believe what I was hearing. I was to prepare a sermon to reflect the worst day in American history.

I had an evening service to prepare for in Detroit, where I was facing people who had just endured this crushing blow. From their stricken faces and fear-filled eyes, I drew my courage to write something that preachers everywhere could use to help these beloved people for whom Christ died.

That night in my hotel room, without my library or binders of notes that I could draw from, I went to scripture and prayed, studied and wrote all night to prepare a sermon entitled, *"What to Do When the Towers Crumble."* The next morning, as promised, I was able to send that message to the leaders from many Christian streams who had been on the conference call. Many of them gave insights and made improvements. By that afternoon, the message, *"What to Do When the Towers Crumble"* was sent around the world from these denominations and missions-sending agencies to hundreds of thousands of pastors.

I call this "living out of the overflow." When we have studied and practiced, ministered and received ministry, when we have lived on the second mile always giving more than required, there is a residual, an overflow, that we can count on which helps us to fulfill the scripture, "be instant in season and out of season." We can exercise the skills and disciplines we have learned in order to minister in a moment for the moment's need.

To illustrate all that we have discussed in this book, I am closing with this message, "What to Do When the Towers Crumble." It may not be the best sermon I have ever written, but it certainly was the most memorable.

WHAT TO DO WHEN THE TOWERS CRUMBLE

September 11, 2001 will be one of the bloodiest days in United States history. Our two biggest and tallest office towers in New York City were obliterated, and the Pentagon, a symbol and headquarters of our military authority, was ripped open like an egg carton. Our commercial jetliners were turned into weapons of mass murder. We had to stop doing things we always do, from trading stocks, to shopping at the local grocery store or mall, or even to going to Disney World.

On this day, people ran through the ash-covered streets of lower Manhattan like extras in a nuclear winter fantasy, chased by a mighty cloud of dust and debris from the office towers they once occupied. Others, many on fire, jumped from thirty, forty, and even one hundred stories above. One couple, among many of them, clasped hands as they leapt. It is estimated that thousands more died within hours.

Even if September 11, 2001, was not our deadliest day, it was surely our worst. Americans are talking of a "second Pearl Harbor" and "an act of war," but even those comparisons falter. The events of this time are "unspeakable" and are "incomparable."

What do we do when the towers crumble? What do we do when horrific events come to our personal lives and to our nation? What is a biblical response to this national calamity? In days like these we are reminded what Isaiah said centuries ago:

In the day of great slaughter, when the towers fall, streams of water will flow on every high mountain and every lofty hill. The moon will shine like the sun, and the sunlight will be seven times brighter, like the light of seven full days, when the LORD binds up the bruises of his people and heals the wounds he inflicted. (Isa 30: 25-26 NIV).

In the midst of the national tragedy, we humbly suggest several biblical responses:

WE NEED TO REPENT OF OUR PAST PATH OF SIN
(Isa 30: 1-14)

Our choices have consequences. Our rebellion has results. In many ways, the results of the recent days are a reflection of the crumbling foundation of America. It is time to reflect and repent. It is time to rend our hearts and not our garments.

We Need to Repent of the Rejection of God's Word (v. 1).

We have carried out plans that are not pleasing to the Lord. We have formed ungodly alliances that are most dishonorable to God.

As a nation, we have heard God's words over and over, and yet we have ignored them. We have insulted God. The highest court in our land has forced the Ten Commandment out of our schools and has forbidden little children to pray and read God's Word. America has flooded the world with unimaginable perversion on the Internet and through films and television.

We have given legal protection to conduct that God calls an abomination, and worse than these things, we have slaughtered up to 40 million innocent babies in the last three decades. As a nation, we have told Almighty God that He is no longer welcome in our public square. We need to plead with God to forgive us and restore in us a holy fear and reverence for God's commands.

We Need to Repent of the Rejection of God's Wisdom (vv.2-8).

We have trusted more in our land than in our Lord, more in our gold and silver, than in our God and Savior. It has brought shame and disgrace upon our nation. We cannot expect the Lord to protect us until we turn back to Him. We need to sincerely pray, "God, please forgive us, cleanse us and help us to trust you."

We need to trust more in our Creator than in creation, more in God's Word than in man's wisdom. It has been said, "God is our greatest hope and our greatest threat." It is time to repent of our past path of sin.

We Need to Repent for the Rejection of God's Will (vv. 9-14).

Our rebellion is bringing us destruction and allowing our enemies to triumph over us. We need to pray that God will restore the walls of His protection around our nation. Over the years, God has sent his message and his messengers, but as a nation we have chosen not to listen to the truth. We must always remember that facts may make us smart, but truth will set us free. We are thankful for the Statue Of Liberty in New York City's harbor, but we also need a Statue of Responsibility in San Francisco's harbor. We need to pray that God will grant to us continued liberty, combined with responsibility. Second, when the towers crumble,

WE NEED TO REMEMBER OUR PRESENT PROBLEMS
(Isa 30:15-18)

Could we not be living through the experience of Samson described in Judges 16:20, when he sought, "I will do as before and shake myself free. But he did not know that the Lord had left him."

This national tragedy provides an opportunity for the Church to serve our people. This is a defining moment for the Church. We need to bind up the wounded, minister to the brokenhearted, encourage the despondent and lead people to Jesus Christ. We must instruct, illustrate, and inspire others by our words, works, witness, and worship in times of great, heart wrenching tragedy.

We need to move from a natural response to a supernatural response. We must resist the temptation to step down from the heavenly level to a human level. As Christians, our goal is not "an eye for an eye and a tooth for a tooth." God says, "In repentance and rest is your salvation, in quietness and trust is your strength..." (Isa 30: 15).

We must remember that our strength is found waiting on the Lord. We must not try to flee from our problems. Instead of trying to run from our enemies, we must run to the Lord. Yet the LORD longs to be gracious to you; he rises to show you compassion. For the LORD is a God of justice. Blessed are all who wait for him! (Isa 30:18 NIV).

What are some practical responses that we can apply in the days ahead?

We Need to Pray for Divine Intervention from God.

We need to pray for those who govern our nation. We need to pray for our President, George W. Bush, his entire cabinet, and for Congress. We need to bombard heaven with intercession, requesting that God grant our national, political leaders discernment and direction. We need to pray for the victims who are suffering in hospitals and for families who have lost their love ones through this horrific event. We need to pray for peace in our world.

We Need to Provide Compassionate Ministry in Behalf of the Lord.

We encourage you to get involved in the lives of people who are hurting as a result of this terrorism. People will need shelter, clothing, food and water, money, and counseling. If you know of someone who has been affected by the most recent events, then reach out to them. Do not wait for them to reach out to you. We must be proactive in these days.

Third, when the towers crumble,

WE NEED TO RECLAIM OUR PRECIOUS PROMISES
(Isa 30: 19-33)

God can turn tragedy into triumph! It is time to reclaim the promises of God. If we turn to Him, He will turn our weeping into singing (v. 19). God desires to answer our prayers.

In the midst of national calamity, God is going to send us godly teachers to instruct us in all aspects of our lives. If we listen carefully, we will hear the voice of the Lord saying, *"Whether you turn right or to the left, your ears will hear a voice behind you, saying, 'This is the way, walk in it'"*(vv. 20-21 NIV).

We Need to Reclaim the Promises of National Revival.

We must shake ourselves from all spiritual sleep and wake up to the awesome presence of God. God is sounding the final alarm. We must not hit the snooze button and go back to sleep again.

We need to pray as the psalmist prayed: "Wilt Thou not Thyself revive us again, that thy people may rejoice in Thee? Show us Thy loving kindness, O Lord, and grant us Thy salvation." (Ps. 85: 6-7 KJV). We need to believe that through these events that God will spark the flames of revival and spread them by the wind of his Holy Spirit.

We Need to Re-Emphasize Prayer as a First Defense, Not a Last Resort.

I am talking about the arithmetic of prayer, or how many times you pray. I am talking about the geometry of prayer, or how long your prayers may be. I am talking about the music of prayer or how sweet your voice may be to God. I am not speaking about rhetoric of prayer or the words you may choose. I am not talking about the logic of prayer or the kind of argumentation you may use to touch the heart of God.

We Need to Restructure Our Priorities in the Eyes of God.

God desires to move us away from our national idolatry (v. 22) to prosper our nation once again (vv. 23-24). He longs to bless to America. As stated earlier, God's Word says, "In the day of great slaughter, when the towers fall, streams of water will flow on every high mountain and every lofty hill. The moon will shine like the sun, and the sunlight will be seven times brighter, like the light of seven full days, when the LORD binds up the bruises of his people and heals the wounds he inflicted (vv. 25-26 NIV).

We believe that God is in the midst of shaking the world in order to bring glory to his name (vv. 27-28). The Holy Spirit will give us a song to sing in the night (v. 29). Even though the towers may crumble, God will cause his majestic voice to be heard throughout the earth (vv. 30-33).

We Need to Rely on the Providence of God in Our Every Day Lives (Isa 50: 10:11)

The events of September 11, 2001 have shocked and rocked the world. The forces of evil have invaded the city and country that have welcomed the world with the great promise of freedom, safety, and security. In these horrific times, we must respond by faith, not fear; in hope, not despair; with love, not hate; with humility, not pride; with action, not apathy.

When King Jehoshaphat was told a vast army was coming against him, he was alarmed and immediately determined to seek the Lord. He called his people together and prayed the following prayer. We encourage you to pray:

"O Lord, God of our fathers, are you not the God who is in heaven? You rule over all the kingdoms of the nations. Power and might are in your hand, and no one can withstand you…if calamity comes upon us, whether the sword of judgment, or plague or famine, we will stand in your presence before the temple that bears your Names and will cry out to you in our distress, and you will hear us and save us…we don't know what to do, but our eyes are upon you."

Then, the Word of God says, *"Then they stood up and praised the Lord, the God of Israel, with a very loud voice.… Jehoshaphat appointed men to sing to the Lord and to praise him for the splendor of his holiness…saying, 'Give thanks to the Lord, for his love endures forever!' As they began to sing and praise, the Lord set ambushes against the men of Ammon and Moab and Mt. Seir who were invading Judah, and they were defeated"* (2 Chr 20:19-22)

When the towers crumble, we need to repent of our past path of sin, we need to remember our present problems, and we need to reclaim our precious promises.

When we prepare a little extra and go the extra mile, then when we are called upon in a crisis or do not have much time to prepare, we can draw truth from the overflow of our lives. I challenge you as a fellow preacher of the gospel to prepare and preach your sermons for the greatest One in your audience, our Lord and Savior Jesus Christ. He listens to our every word, and one day we will give an account as to how we have rightly divided the Word of God.

CONCLUSION

Of this church I was made a minister according to the stewardship from God bestowed on me for your benefit so that I might fully carry out the preaching of the word of God. (Col 1:25)

And He ordered us to preach to the people, and solemnly to testify that this is the One who has been appointed by God as Judge of the living and the dead. (Acts 10:42)

Gutenbergers and Googlers are called to "preach the Word" and to be ready "in season and out of season." We are commanded to be faithful when it is not popular, even when it is painful. We are to preach not just the passages that are easy but also hard, not just those we like but those that bring us to our knees. If you are a Gutenberger, you have been challenged to broaden your communication horizon to connect with the Googler as well as your own tribe. This takes more than having a contemporary worship service to accomplish! If you are a Googler, you have been stretched to communicate to both to the Gutenbergers and Googlers without watering down the Gospel. We are not called to just select the biblical images that we easily relate to or to speak from the pericopes, or passages, we can comprehend quickly. Regardless of what tribe we were born in, the end result is for people's lives to be saved through Jesus Christ.

For both Gutenbergers and Googlers to be relevant in a secular society, the whole brain must be energized in the preparation and presentation process. There are three all-encompassing questions that must be answered before presenting the gospel today:

1. **What is the point of the passage?** This is accomplished through investigation, interpretation and illumination by the preacher.
2. **What are the pictures for the people?** Creativity and imagination build the bridge from the ancient text to the present day.
3. **What is the package for the preacher?** The preacher will have to decide, based on the audience, exactly how the message is to be structured for maximum results.

The great early American preacher, Phillips Brooks, defined preaching as the "communication of divine truth through human personality." One of my seminary preaching professors boiled down Brook's definition to three words, "Preaching is you" (Brooks, 43).

No two preachers are alike. We may employ different preferences as to the distinctives of our presentations. Or, to the mannerism of preaching—enthusiastic or conversational. Some preach longer and others shorter. But, whatever style or type of preaching we employ, we seek for the anointing of God's Spirit to be on our preaching ministry.

The end result of preaching is that people come to Christ, have their walk in Him deepened, and their lives changed by the application of God's Word through the power of the Holy Spirit.

Gutenberg to Google: The Twenty Indispensable Laws of Communication was written to help you with instruction, inspiration, and insight so that your own unique preaching ministry can be enriched, expanded and empowered. The emphasis indeed is on "you." How can your preaching preparation and delivery be further honed and developed so that you can be more effective than ever in the proclamation of God's Word?

One of my favorite quotes on preaching was passed on to me by Dr. George O. Wood, the General Superintendent of the Assemblies of God, written in the January 27, 1917, issue of *The Weekly Evangel*, predecessor to *The Pentecostal Evangel*, entitled "A Few Hints to Preachers."

If you do not want to "break," make your shirt collar an inch larger, and give your blood a chance to flow back to the heart. Do not get excited too soon. Do not run away from your hearers. Engine driving-wheels fly fast with no load, but when they draw anything they go slower.

It takes a cold hammer to bend a hot iron. Heat up the people, but keep the hammer cold. Do not bawl and scream. Too much water stops mill-wheels, and too much noise drowns sense. Empty vessels ring loudest. Powder isn't shot. Thunder isn't lightning. Lightning kills. If you have lightning, you can afford to thunder; but do not try to thunder out of an empty cloud.

The best preachers are not "thunder from an empty cloud" but are part of the noblest calling on earth, to draw others into communion with Jesus, the Christ, the Savior of the world. This world and God's Church needs powerful preachers for the 21st century. Our prayer is that this resource becomes a valuable tool for you to be all the preacher God wants you to be! God sent His Son to save both Gutenbergers and Googlers.

BIBLIOGRAPHY

Achtemeir, Elizabeth. *Creative Preaching.* Nashville: Abingdon, 1980.

Arredondo, Lani. *How to Present Like a Pro: Getting People to See Things Your Way.* New York: McGraw-Hill, 1991.

Avens, Robert. *Imagination Is Reality.* Dallas: Spring Publications, 1980.

Baumann, J. Daniel. *An Introduction to Contemporary Preaching.* Grand Rapids: Baker, 1972.

Beecher, Henry Ward. *Yale's Lectures on Preaching.* New York: J. B. Ford and Company, 1872.

Blackaby, Henry and Tom Blackaby. *The Man God Uses.* Nashville: Broadman and Holman, 1999.

Bounds, E. M. *Powerful and Prayerful Pulpit.* Grand Rapids: Baker, 1993.

Bright, Bill. *The Coming Revival: America's Call to Fast, and Pray, and "Seek God's Face."* Orlando: New Life, 1995.

Bright, Bill and James Davis. *Beyond All Limits The Synergistic Church For A Planet in Crisis.* Atlanta: New Life, 2002.

Brembeck, Winston and William Howell. *Persuasion: A Means Of Social Influence.* Englewood Cliffs: Prentice-Hall, Inc., 1976.

Broadus, John A. *On the Preparation and the Delivery of Sermons.* 4th ed. San Francisco: Harper and Row, 1979.

Brooks, Peter. *Communicating Conviction.* London: Epworth Press, 1983.

Brown, Charles Reynolds. *The Art of Preaching.* New York: Macmillan, 1922.

Bugg, Charles B. *Preaching From the Inside Out.* Nashville: Broadman, 1992.

Bunyan, John. *Pilgrims Progress*, 1678

Buttrick, David. *A Captive Voice*. Louisville: Westminster/John Knox Press, 1994.

Buttrick, George A. *Jesus Came Preaching*. 2nd ed. Grand Rapids: Baker, 1970.

Chapell, Bryan. *Christ Centered Preaching: Redeeming The Expository Sermon*, 2005. Place and publisher?

Coleman, Robert. *The Master Plan of Evangelism*. 3rd ed. Old Tappan: Revell, 1981.

Coulson, John. *Religion and Imagination*. Oxford: The Clarendon Press?, 1981.

Dale, R. W. *Nine Lectures on Preaching*. London: Hodder and Stoughton, 1986.

Davis, James O. *The Pastor's Best Friend: The New Testament Evangelist*. Springfield, MO: Gospel Publishing House, 1997.

Davis, Grady. H. *Design For Preaching*. Philadelphia: Fortress Press, 1958.

Decker, Bert. *You Have To Believed To Be Heard*. New York: Saint Martin's Press, 1992

Dixon, John W., Jr. *Art and the Theological Imagination*. New York: Seabury, 1978.

Duduit, Michael. *Handbook of Contemporary Preaching*. Nashville, Broadman, 1992.

Egan, Kieran. *Imagination in Teaching and Learning*. Chicago: University of Chicago, 1992.

Fish, Roy J. *Giving an Effective Invitation*. Nashville: Broadman, 1974.

Flynn, Leslie B. *Come Alive With Illustrations*. Grand Rapids: Baker, 1987.

Fridman, Thomas L. *The World Is Flat*. New York: Farrar, Straus and Giroux, 2005.

Freeman, Harold. *Variety in Biblical Preaching*. Waco: Word Books, 1987.
Frye, Northrop. *The Educated Imagination*. Bloomington: Indiana University, 1964.

_____. *Words With Power*. New York: Harcourt Brace Jovanovich, 1990.

Ghiselin, Brewster (ed.). *The Creative Process*. Berkeley: University of California, 1985.

Greenleaf, Robert K. *On Becoming a Servant Leader*. San Francisco: Jossey-Bass Publishers, 1996.

Greidanus, Sidney. *The Modern Preacher and the Ancient Text*. Grand Rapids: Eerdmans, 1988.

Gruden, Robert. *The Grace of Great Things: Creativity and Innovation*. New York: Ticknor and Fields, 1990.

Hawkes, Terence. *Metaphor*. London: Methuen, 1972.

Hendricks, Howard G. *Teaching to Change Lives*. Portland: Multnomah Press, 1987.

Hendricks, Howard and William Hendricks. *As Iron Sharpens Iron*. Chicago: Moody, 1994.

Hoff, Ron. *I Can See You Naked*. Kansas City: Andrews and McMeel, 1992.

Holmes, Urban T., III. *Ministry and Imagination*. New York: Seabury, 1976.

Hull, William E. "The Contemporary World and the Preaching Task." In Michael Duduit (ed.) *Handbook of Contemporary Preaching*. Nashville: Broadman, 1992.

Hunter, George G. *How to Reach Secular People*. Nashville: Abingdon, 1992.

Hutchcraft, Ronald. "Relating the Gospel to a Secular Society." In Lewis A. Drummond's (ed.) *Equipping for Evangelism*. Minneapolis: World Wide Publications, 1996.

Huttar, Charles (ed.). *Imagination and the Spirit*. Grand Rapids: Baker, 1971.

Jeary, Tony. *Inspire Any Audience*. Tulsa, Trade Life, 1997

Kaiser, Walter C. *Toward An Exegetical Theology*. Grand Rapids: Baker, 1981.

Kendall, R. T. *Stand Up and Be Counted: Calling for a Public Confession of Faith*. Grand Rapids: Zondervan, 1985.

Kirkpatrick, Robert White. *The Creative Delivery of Sermons*. New York: Macmillan, 1944.

Kuhlman, Edward. *The Master Teacher*. Old Tappan: Revell, 1987.

Larsen, David. *The Anatomy of Preaching*. Grand Rapids: Baker, 1989.

_____. *The Company Of The Preachers*. Grand Rapids: Kregel, 1998.

_____. *The Evangelism Mandate—Recovering the Centrality of Gospel Preaching.* Wheaton: Crossway Books, 1992.

Larson, Brian, and Mark Galli. *Preaching That Connects.* Grand Rapids: Zondervan, 1994.

Lewis, David. *How to Get Your Message Across.* London: Souvenir Press, 1996.

Lewis, Ralph L., and Gregg Lewis. *Learning to Preach like Jesus.* Westchester: Crossway Books, 1989.

Loscalzo, Craig A. *Evangelistic Preaching That Connects.* Downers Grove: InterVarsity, 1995.

MacArthur, John. *How To Preaching Biblically,* Moody: 2005

MacArthur, John. *The MacArthur New Testament Commentary: Ephesians.* Chicago: Moody, 1986.

_____. *Rediscovering Expository Preaching.* Waco: Word Books, 1992.

Mackay, Harvey. *Beware The Man Who Offers You His Shirt.* New York: Fawcett Columbine, 1990.

_____. *Swim With The Sharks Without Being Eaten Alive.* New York: Fawcett Columbine, Ballantine Books, 1988.

McDill, Wayne. *12 Essential Skills for Great Preaching,* 2006.

McLaughlin, Raymond W. *The Ethics of Persuasive Preaching.* Grand Rapids: Baker. 1979.

Olford, Stephen. *Anointed Expository Preaching.* Broadman: Nashville, 1998.

Osborne, Grant. *The Hermeneutical Spiral.* Downers Grove: InterVarsity Press, 1991.

Palmer, Richard E. *Hermeneutics.* Evanston, Illinois: Northwestern University, 1969.

Patterson, Ben. "Preaching and Prayer." In Michael Duduit (ed.) *Communicate With Power.* Grand Rapids: Baker, 1996.

Pattison, T. Harwood. *The Making of the Sermon.* Philadelphia: The American Baptist Publications Society, 1898.

Perry, Lloyd M. *Biblical Preaching for Today's World.* Chicago: Moody, 1973.

Perry, Lloyd M., and John R. Strubhar. *Evangelistic Preaching*. Chicago: Moody, 1979.

Piper, John. *The Supremacy of God In Preaching*. Grand Rapids: Baker, 1990.

Phillips, John. *Only One Life*. Neptune: Loizeaux, 1995.

Quayle, William A. *The Pastor-Preacher*. New York: Eaton and Mains, 1910.

Qubein, Nido R. *How to Be a Great Communicator*. New York: John Wiley and Sons, 1997.

_____. *Stairway to Success*. New York: John Wiley and Sons, 1997.

Rice, Charles L. *Interpretation and Imagination*. Philadelphia: Fortress, 1970.

Robinson, Haddon W. *Biblical Preaching*. Grand Rapids: Baker, 1980.

_____. *Biblical Sermons*. Grand Rapids: Baker, 1989.

_____. *Making A Difference in Preaching*. Grand Rapids: Baker, 1999.

Salter, Darius. *American Evangelism*. Grand Rapids: Baker, 1996.

Simpson, Matthew. *Yale's Lectures on Preaching*. New York: Hunt and Eaton, 1879.

Spurgeon, Charles H. *The Soul Winner*. Grand Rapids: Eerdmans, 1963.

_____. *Lectures to My Students*. Grand Rapids: Baker, 1977.

Stanley, Andy. *Communicating for a Change: Seven Keys To Irresistible Communication*. 2007

Stott, John R. W. *The Preacher's Portrait*. Grand Rapids: Eerdmans, 1961.

_____. *God's New Society*. Downers Grove: InterVarsity, 1979.
_____. *Between Two Worlds*. Grand Rapids: Eerdmans, 1982.

Street, Alan R. *The Effective Invitation*. Old Tappan: Revell, 1984.

Sweet, Leonard. *Aqua Church*. Loveland: Group, 1999.

Sunukjian, Don. *Invitation To Biblical Preaching: Proclaiming The Truth With Clairity And Relevance*, 2007.

Sweeting, George. *The Evangelistic Camp*. Chicago: Moody, 1955.

Taylor, Jack R. *The Word of God With Power*. Nashville: Broadman, 1993.

Troeger, Thomas H. *Imagining a Sermon*. Nashville: Abingdon, 1990.

Vance, Mike and Diane Deacon. *Think Out of the Box*. Franklin Lakes, NJ: Career Press, 1996.

Vines, Jerry. *A Practical Guide to Sermon Preparation*. Chicago: Moody, 1985.

_____. *A Guide to Effective Sermon Delivery*. Chicago: Moody, 1986.

Waitley, Dennis. *The Psychology of Winning*. Niles: Nightingale, 1987.

Warren, Rick. *The Purpose Driven Church*. Grand Rapids: Zondervan, 1995.

Webb, Joseph M. *Preaching Without Notes*, 2001

White, Douglas M. *The Excellence of Exposition*. Neptune: Loizeaux Brothers, 1984.

Whitsell, F. D. *Sixty-Five Ways to Give an Evangelistic Invitation*. Grand Rapids: Kregel Publications, 1984.

Wiersbe, Warren W. *Preaching and Teaching with Imagination: The Quest for Biblical Preaching*. Wheaton: Victor Books, 1994.

Wilkinson, Bruce H. *The Seven Laws of the Learner*. Sisters, OR: Multnomah Press, 1992.

Wilson, Paul Scott. *Imagination of the Heart—New Understanding in Preaching*. Nashville: Abingdon, 1988.

Young, Robert D. *Religious Imagination: God's Gift to Prophets and Preachers*. Philadelphia: Westminster, 1979.

ABOUT THE AUTHOR

Dr. James O. Davis founded Cutting Edge International and co-founded the Billion Soul Network, a growing coalition of more than 750 Christian ministries and denominations synergizing their efforts to build the premier community of pastors worldwide to help plant five million new churches for a billion soul harvest. The Billion Soul Network, with more than 200,000 churches, has become the largest pastors network in the world.

Christian leaders recognize Dr. Davis as one of the leading networkers in the Christian world. More than 40,000 pastors and leaders have attended his biannual pastors conference and leadership summits across the US and in all major world regions. During 2007-2009, leaders committed to plant more than three million new churches. He has networked with significant leaders from different spheres such as George O. Wood, Jack Hayford, Johnny Hunt, Robert Schuller, D. James Kennedy, Reinhard Bonnke, Chuck Norris, Charles Blake, Barry Black and others.

Dr. Davis served twelve years leading 1500 evangelists and training thousands of students for full-time evangelism as the National Evangelists Representative at the Assemblies of God world headquarters. Ministering more than 45 weeks per year for 25 years to an average yearly audience of 100,000 people, Dr. Davis has now traveled nearly seven million miles to minister face-to-face to more than 5,000,000 people in nearly 100 nations.

Dr. Davis earned a Doctorate in Ministry in Preaching at Trinity Evangelical Divinity School and two master's degrees from the Assemblies of God Theological Seminary. As an author and editor, he has provided: *The Pastor's Best Friend: The New Testament Evangelist; Living Like Jesus; The Preacher's Summit; Gutenberg to Google: The Twenty Indispensable Laws of Communication.* He co-authored with Dr. Bill Bright, *Beyond All Limits: The Synergistic Church for a Planet in Crisis.* His quotes and articles have appeared in *Charisma, Ministry Today, The Challenge Weekly, New York Times Magazine,* and elsewhere.

Dr. Davis resides in the Orlando area with his wife, Sheri, and daughters, Olivia and Priscilla. They have two children, Jennifer and James, who reside in heaven.

James O. Davis may be invited to speak for your church or organization by contacting:

James O. Davis
Billion Soul
P. O. Box 411605
Melbourne, Florida 32941-1605
(417) 861-9999
www.JamesODavis.org